Public Worship
Considered & Enforced

Joseph Kinghorn

Public Worship
Considered & Enforced

Edited and Introduced by Baiyu Andrew Song
Foreword by Matthew Boswell

IN PARTNERSHIP WITH

CENTRE for BAPTIST STUDIES
at HERITAGE THEOLOGICAL SEMINARY

Public Worship Considered and Enforced

Copyright © 2020 H&E Publishing
www.hesedandemet.com

Published by: H&E Publishing, Peterborough, Canada
The Andrew Fuller Centre for Baptist Studies at Heritage Theological Seminary, Cambridge, Canada

All rights reserved. This book or any portion thereof may not be reproduced or used in any manner whatsoever without the express written permission of the publisher except for the use of brief quotations in a book review.

Unless otherwise indicated, all Scripture quotations are from The ESV® Bible (The Holy Bible, English Standard Version®), copyright © 2001 by Crossway, a publishing ministry of Good News Publishers. Used by permission. All rights reserved.

Source in Public Domain: Joseph Kinghorn, *Public Worship: Considered and Enforced*. Printed in Norwich. R. Bacon, 1800.

Cover Image: *The Preaching of Saint John the Baptist in the Wilderness*, Pieter Brueghel the Younger (1564–1638).

Paperback ISBN: 978-1-989174-43-2
eBook ISBN: 978-1-989174-44-9
First Edition, 2020

"Standing in a long line of Baptist heroes, Joseph Kinghorn maintains that public worship is of vital interest to Christian religion. Baiyu Andrew Song has done a great service to the church in editing this forgotten work on public worship. Kinghorn offers many doctrinal and practical insights into why public worship matters. In an age where individualism runs rampant, he exhorts us to see that faithfulness to public worship bears witness to our love for God as well as our love for fellow believers. I highly commend this treasure from Baptist history to you in remembering why our gathering together to worship matters."

—**Jake Stone**, Pastor, New Testament Baptist Church, Biloxi, MS

"Through dint of research and reading, Prof. Baiyu Song has become a leading expert on the life and ministry of the late-eighteenth-century English Baptist Joseph Kinghorn. Quite unknown to the majority of his Baptist descendants today, this pastor-theologian very much deserves to be read and appreciated, and his tract on worship is the ideal place to begin. I am thrilled to see it, as well as Prof. Song's fine introduction to Kinghorn and the tract, in print."
—**Michael A.G. Haykin**, Chair and Professor of Church History, The Southern Baptist Theological Seminary, Louisville, KY; Director of The Andrew Fuller Center for Baptist Studies

"I am grateful to my friend, Baiyu Song, for the re-presentation of Joseph Kinghorn's work on public worship. Kinghorn sought to write clearly and concisely so that his work 'might have the chance of circulating and being read,' and did so because he cared deeply about the glory of God and the building up of his church. Kinghorn's work is especially needed today as it reorients the church to the important place of public worship in the life of the Christian."
—**Devon Kauflin**, Pastor, Grace Church, Clarksburg, MD; Assistant Director, Sovereign Grace Music

"A beautiful and timeless challenge—to the individualism that pervades self and culture—that corporate worship is vital for a healthy biblical spirituality."
—**Natalie Brand**, Author, *Complementarian Spirituality: Reformed Women and Union with Christ*

"Church history contains many spiritual treasures, and they are waiting for men and women of later generations to discover. I appreciate Baiyu Andrew Song leading us to mine this treasure through the life and work of Joseph Kinghorn. Kinghorn unfolds the rich spiritual meaning of public worship through this book from the individual level to the level of the kingdom of God. His Christ-centered, pastoral, and pious thinking on public worship is what modern ministers urgently need."
   —**Boaz W. Yang**, Director, Praise as One Ministry (laijingbai.com)

"If you want to know how the duty of honoring the Lord's Day can become a delight, you should read Joseph Kinghorn's *Public Worship Considered & Enforced*. Baiyu A. Song does a good job at drawing our attention to the life and writings of Kinghorn which is indeed 'a rich spiritual mine.' The importance of believers gathering for corporate worship (Heb. 10:25) is as crucial today as it was in the early church and in Kinghorn's day; his short book surprised me by its theological depth, use of Scripture, and practical guide in its treatment of the subject."
   —**Osmond J. Jerome**, Senior Pastor, Christie Street Baptist Church; Adjunct Professor, Toronto Baptist Seminary & Bible College

...not neglecting to meet together,
as is the habit of some...
Hebrews 10:25

To

Rev. Haddon A. Haynes,
Ms Mabel Baker,
and Mrs Ruby Price

pastoral mentor, spiritual mother, and example of Christian love

A Note from the Editor

"Editing should be, especially in the case of old writers, a counselling rather than a collaborating task. The tendency of the writer-editor to collaborate is natural, but he should say to himself, 'How can I help this writer to say it better in his own style?' and avoid 'How can I show him how I would write it, if it were my piece?'" These are invaluable advices from the twentieth-century cartoonist and author James Thurber (1894–1961). Such a principle is applied when I transcribed and edited Joseph Kinghorn's *Public Worship Considered and Enforced*. While trying to preserve much of Kinghorn's text, this edition also seeks to serve the contemporary readers for their reading and understanding. In its eighteenth-century edition, Kinghorn's *Public Worship* was printed as a single piece without chapter divisions. Furthermore, all scriptural quotations were from the King James Version. In this modern edition, I have divided the work into chapters. Since fewer Christians read the King James Version today, I decided to replace all scriptural quotations with the English Standard Version. Linguistically, these two versions are quite similar, and readers will not find inconsistency while reading this text. Furthermore, a few footnotes are also provided for the readers' benefit.

CONTENTS

FOREWORD xvii
Matthew Boswell

INTRODUCTION 1
Baiyu Andrew Song

ORIGINAL PREFACE 25

Public Worship Considered and Enforced

1. A CREATURE'S DUTY 27
2. KNOWING GOD & OURSELVES 31
3. A MEANS OF WITNESS 35
4. CHRISTIAN DISCIPLESHIP & COMFORT 41
5. THE CITY OF GOD REVEALED 45
6. APPLICATIONS 51

APPENDIX 1: A CHRONOLOGY OF JOSEPH KINGHORN'S PUBLICATIONS 61

APPENDIX II: A POEM BY DAVID KINGHORN 65

SCRIPTURE INDEX 69

Foreword

Matthew Boswell

The earliest record of a Baptist worship service occurs in a letter from Hughe and Anne Bromhead in 1609. They chronicle two Sunday services of worship which lasted three to four hours each in length. The gathering is described as beginning with prayer, followed by the reading of a chapter or two from the Scripture. Prayer would then be offered preceding the preaching of the word. After the preacher concluded his approximately forty-five-minute sermon, there was more time of prayer, followed by various other sermons that would be given until the time had expired. The first preacher would then rise again at the conclusion of the service to conduct a final exhortation, encourage the congregation to give to the poor, and offer an adjourning prayer of benediction.[1] Though this free-church liturgy would adapt and change with the ever-mutable political and societal current in the years that followed, the essential practices contained in the worship of the early Baptists would serve as a foundation for successive congregations even to the modern era.

---

[1] Champion Burrage, *The Early English Dissenters in Light of Recent Research, 1550-1641* (Cambridge: Cambridge University Press, 1912), 2:176–177. Also see Leon McBeth, *The Baptist Heritage* (Nashville: Broadman, 1987), 91.

PUBLIC WORSHIP

This early first-hand description illuminates how intentionally distinct Baptist order of worship was from other denominations. The best articulation of which ordinances would have been present in a Baptist service is given in the *Second London Confession of Faith* (1677/1689):

> The reading of the Scriptures, preaching, and hearing the Word of God, teaching and admonishing one another in Psalms, hymns, and spiritual songs, singing with grace in your hearts to the Lord; as to the administration of baptism, and the Lord's supper, are all parts of religious worship of God, to be performed in obedience to him, with understanding, faith, reverence, and godly fear.[2]

The Baptists understood the formational impact of corporate worship and, to that end, were in pursuit of a thorough biblical faithfulness matched with purity of devotion in every administration.

The first time I heard the name Joseph Kinghorn beyond a footnote was in a doctoral seminar given by Baiyu Song on biblical spirituality. I believe his passion to research and communicate his findings on this overlooked father in Baptist history is a worthy endeavour and has been an encouragement to my own continued study. In the midst of the complexities of English Baptist ecclesiology and doxological tensions, Song serves as a capable guide in understanding how this new sect could make its way forward to become a thriving movement.

---

[2] *Second London Confession of Faith* 22.5.

INTRODUCTION

Though removed from modern readers by history, I believe this volume re-presenting Joseph Kinghorn's *Public Worship* contains valuable pastoral benefit for us today, and hope that the passion Kinghorn demonstrates for the worship of God spreads to our generation. I pray further that such passion be done "according to the book," and goes on to spark renewal in all matters of Christian worship.

Matthew Boswell
Hymnwriter;
Pastor, The Trails Church, Prosper, TX;
Assistant Professor of Christian Worship,
The Southern Baptist Theological Seminary

Used with kind permission of the Angus Library and Archives, Regent's Park College, Oxford University

INTRODUCTION

Baiyu Andrew Song

When Raymond Brown published his *The English Baptists of the Eighteenth Century*, he included a copy of an old print.[1] According to Roger Hayden (1936-2016), this print which "used to hang in chapel vestries, was a composite etching of Baptist worthies at the opening of the Victorian period, gathered round a vestry table."[2] Based on previous individual portraits, the unknown artist assembled fifteen advocates of Baptist oversea missions in one scene.[3] The value of this assemblage is historical, as it represents the legacy of these early directors of the Baptist missions and how the following generation remembered them.

---

[1] Raymond Brown, *The English Baptists of the Eighteenth Century*, A History of the English Baptists, vol. 2 (London: The Baptist Historical Society, 1986).

[2] Roger Hayden, *English Baptist History and Heritage*, 2nd ed. (Didcot, Oxon: The Baptist Union of Great Britain, 2005), 128.

[3] Beside the five missionaries—William Carey (1761-1834), Joshua Marshman (1768-1837), William Ward (1769-1823), William Knibb (1803-1845), and Thomas Burchell (1799-1846); seven Particular Baptist ministers (Joseph Kinghorn [1766-1832], John Rippon [1751-1836], John Ryland, Jr. [1753-1825], Robert Hall, Jr. [1764-1831], Andrew Fuller [1754-1815], William Steadman [1765-1837], and Samuel Pearce [1766-1799]); two General Baptist ministers (Dan Taylor [1738-1816] and J. G. Pike [1784-1854]); and a Baptist essayist (John Foster [1770-1843]) are in the print. Curiously, only four of these men attended the initiative meeting of the Society on October 2, 1792 at Mrs. Beeby Wallis' parlour in Kettering. The four attendants include Carey, Ryland, Fuller, Pearce, Reynold Hogg of Trapstone, John Sutcliff of Olney, Abraham Greenwood of Oakham, Edward Sharman of Cottisbrook, Joseph Timms of Kettering, Joshua Burton of Foxton, Thomas Blundel of Arnsby, William Heighton of Roade, John Ayres of Braybrook, William Staughton of Bristol, and a theological student at Bristol Academy.

Artistically, John Ryland, Jr. (1753-1825) is positioned in the middle of the print and the "v" shape created by John Rippon (1751-1836) and Dan Taylor (1738-1816) behind Ryland confirms his significance, at least in the artist's mind. Furthermore, among the five seated figures, Joseph Kinghorn (1766-1832) is the only one who has an open book in his hand. Both Kinghorn's right hand (thus his book) and his right leg direct the viewer's eyes toward the only standing figure in the front row, Robert Hall, Jr. (1764-1831). Similarly, Hall's right hand also holds an open book, and he directs it toward Kinghorn. Such an arrangement allows us to interpret that the decade-long controversy (1815-1827) between Hall and Kinghorn— former tutor and student, second cousins twice removed, and friends—over the terms of communion had been left unsolved among the English Baptists.[4]

---

[4] See Peter Naylor, *Calvinism, Communion and the Baptists: A Study of English Calvinistic Baptists from the Late 1600s to the Early 1800s* (Carlisle, Cambria; Waynesboro, GA: Paternoster, 2003) and Kenneth Dix, *Strict and Particular: English Strict and Particular Baptists in the Nineteenth Century* (Didcot, Oxon: The Baptist Historical Society for the Strict Baptist Historical Society, 2001). In the case of Kinghorn's own church in Norwich, a legal suit was filed over the term of communion in early Victorian era, see William Norton, ed., *Baptist Chapel, St. Mary's, Norwich. The Suit—Attorney-General versus Gould and Others, in the Rolls Court: Its Origin, the Proceedings, Pleadings, and Judgment* (London: Houlston and Wright, 1860). On American views on the issue, see anonymous, "Open Communion Baptists by an American," *Primitive Church (Or Baptist) Magazine* 242 (February 1864): 46-47; Robert Boyte C. Howell, *The Terms of Communion at the Lord's Table*, 2nd ed. (Philadelphia: American Baptist Publication Society, 1846).

The communion controversy was not new, as Baptists of the previous generations also argued over the term of communion. In general, there were two positions regarding who could participate the Lord's Table. On one hand, the Open-Communionists (such as John Bunyan, Robert Robinson, and Hall) believed that since the Lord's Table advocated the communion of saints, all genuine believers could celebrate this ordinance together. In other words, there was no relationship between baptism and the Lord's Table for them. On the other hand, the Strict-Communionists (or Close-Communionists, such as William Kiffin, Abraham Booth, Andrew Fuller, and Kinghorn) believed that for local Baptist congregations, only those who had been baptized as a believer could participate the Lord's

INTRODUCTION

Furthermore, if one reflects on the reasons why Joseph Kinghorn has long been forgotten by contemporary Baptists, the strict-communion position defended by Kinghorn undoubtedly makes readers prejudge him as something of traditional bigot.[5] However, such a view is contrary to how Kinghorn's contemporaries remembered him. For Baptists, Kinghorn's "ardent piety, eminent talents, extensive learning, and distinguished usefulness, endeared him to a wide circle of friends, both of our own and other denominations."[6] To extend this statement, Francis Augustus Cox (1783–1853) commented that

---

Table. Thus, they believed the inseparable relationship between the two ordiances.

[5] This was the case in the nineteenth century, as stated in an article published in the *General Baptist Magazine* in 1871, where it was said that "Let no one weak in faith and hope heave a sigh of despair over the change. If he *must* look back, let him remember how many crosses, how much ignorance, how many sorrows, how much shame, deface the retrospect. Let him think not only the heroic ardour which would have faced the fires of martyrdom for baptism by immersion, or submitted with manly indifference to the robberies of the sheriff's officer that he might demonstrate the sincerity of his protest against church rates, *but of the narrowness which refused to eat bread at the Lord's table with a pædobaptist...*" (italics are original). In response, William Jarrom (1814–1882), an English Baptist missionary in China, wrote that for the strict Communists, "The stand they make in the maintenance of their principles is for the truth's sake. On this account, it is with pain and with a sense of injustice that they find their views and conduct stigmatized as 'narrowness.' They feel that this reflects on some of the founders of the body, whose character for strong intelligence, patience inquiry, caution in forming their opinions, together with firmness in maintaining them, and largeheartedness, stood high while they lived, and is revered in the memory of multitudes now they are dead ... Many thought that Kinghorn had the better of the argument. The present race of Strict Baptists believe that he had, and that he has proved satisfactorily that their views are most in harmony with the teaching and requirements of Christ ... If this be 'narrowness,' it is, according to their mind, the 'narrowness' of the New Testament, of Christ and His apostles, the authors of the plan on which they act—a 'narrowness' for which they are not responsible..." (William Jarrom, "Are Strict Communion Baptists Narrow?," *The General Baptist Magazine* [January 1872]: 22, 23).

[6] J. Belcher, "Baptist Denominational Union Meeting," *The Baptist Magazine* 25 (August 1833): 370.

he had taken a leading part in the proceedings of the Society [i.e., BMS], having moved the first resolution at the unnual [sic] meeting in June, as he had through many years zealously co-operated with the committee. His opinion was always expressed with modesty, and listened to with respect. He was quick in perception; his suggestions were judicious; and in general, he had little of pertinacity. His method of speaking was very similar on the platform and in the pulpit, hurried, partaking of the vivacity of his conceptions, but unformed and inelegant. He had, besides, a kind of jumping, dancing movement, which very much diminished the impression; but he failed not to produce sensible and often ingenious remarks, convincing the hearer that he was possessed of great though not preeminent talents, and that he was deeply in earnest to promote the cause which had engaged his heart. He was possessed of considerable learning, keen as a controversialist, and one of the best biblical critic[s] of the denomination.[7]

Members of Kinghorn's congregation, such as Samuel C. Colman (1825-1911)—a nephew of Jeremiah Colman (1777-1851) who founded Colman Mustard company—recalled:

Mr. Kinghorn's ministry was calculated to make stalwart Bible Christians who knew what they believed and why. In his day there were some sturdy Nonconformists in Norwich, united in close fellowship amongst both Baptists and Independents, who held Mr. Kinghorn in high esteem. In Mr. Kinghorn's early ministry, the city was lighted at night by a few

---

[7] Francis Augustus Cox, *History of the English Baptist Missionary Society, from A.D. 1792 to A.D. 1842* (Boston: Isaac Tompkins, 1844), 172-173.

comparatively miserable oil lamps, and evening meetings were unheard of. Towards the close of his ministry he commenced a Sunday evening meeting, the first ever regularly held in Norwich, and probably after gas lighting had been partially introduced.[8]

Even for the Paedobaptists, as a featured article published in the *Evangelical Magazine* indicated, "though we differed widely from him in his views of strict communion, yet, respecting most highly his Christian virtues and ministerial attainments, we rejoice to testify our love to his memory, by giving publicity to the following particulars."[9]

Unknowingly, but providentially, I have been introduced to David and Joseph Kinghorn by Professor Michael Haykin of The Southern Baptist Theological Seminary during a trip to England in the spring of 2016. Like unknowingly entering a gold mine, I was surprised by precious discoveries through hard but enjoyable labours. My hope here is to introduce you to this rich spiritual mine.

Historical Context
Since the Great Ejection of 1662, the religious situation in England was divided by ecclesial politics—the Church of England and the Dissenting Body existed as two hostile religious entities. Though under the Act of Toleration, limited religious freedom was granted, the Test Act of 1678 was not repealed until 1828, and Dissenters were still subject to restrictions on

---

[8] Helen Caroline Colman, *Jeremiah James Colman: A Memoir* (London: Chiswick, 1905), 18–19.

[9] Anonymous, "Memoir of the Late Rev. Joseph Kinghorn, of Norwich," *The Evangelical Magazine and Missionary Chronicle* 10 (December 1832): 509.

their civil liberties.[10] Politically, the Tory party stood with the established church; thus even in 1811, Henry Addington (1757–1844), then Lord President of the Council, presented the Protestant Dissenting Ministers Bill to the House of Lords.[11] In

---

[10] For a summary of legal acts relate to the Dissenters, see Joseph Beldam, *A Summary of the Laws Peculiarly Affecting Protestant Dissenters. An Appendix, Containing Acts of Parliaments, Trust Deeds, and Legal Forms* (London: Joseph Butterworth and Son, 1827).

The Act of Toleration was published on May 24, 1689 by the Parliament, which abandoned the idea of a "comprehensive" Church of England, and it "allowed Nonconformists their own places of worship and their own teachers and preachers, subject to acceptance of certain oaths of allegiance. Social and political disabilities remained, however, and Nonconformists were still denied political office" (Editors of Encyclopaedia Britannica, "Toleration Act," Encyclopædia Britannica, https://www.britannica.com/event/Toleration-ActGreat-Britain-1689 [accessed on March 17, 2019]).

The Test Act was a law that "made a person's eligibility for public office depend upon his profession of the established religion…The form that the test took in England was to make the receiving of Holy Communion according to the rites of the Church of England a condition precedent to the acceptance of office. It was first embodied in legislation in 1661 as a requisite for membership of a town corporation and was extended to cover all public offices by the Test Act of 1673" (Editors of Encyclopaedia Britannica, "Test Act," Encyclopædia Britannica, https://www.britannica.com/topic/test-act [accessed on March 17, 2019]).

[11] A copy of the bill is made available for access by UK Parliament, and it was summarized as, "the bill was an attempt to provide exemption from military service only to dissenting ministers who were able to be vouched for by six householders, which meant that ministers were unable to speak for their own status" (UK Parliament, "Copy of Lord Sidmouth's Bill Relating to Protestant Dissenting Ministers," HL Deb 09 May 1811 vol 19 cc1133-40, https://api.parliament.uk/historic-hansard/lords/1811/may/09/copy-of-lord-sidmouths-bill-relating-to [accessed on February 12, 2019]). Also see Anonymous, *Remarks on the Failure of Lord Sidmouth's Bill, Relating to Protestant Dissenters* (London, 1811); Charles F. Mullett, "The Legal Position of the English Protestant Dissenters, 1767–1812," *Virginia Law Review* 25.6 (1939): 671–697; Peter Walker, "'A Free and Protestant People'? The Campaign for the Repeal of the Test and Corporation Acts, 1786–1828" (PhD diss., Oxford University, 2010); Michael A. Rutz, "The Problem of Church and State: Dissenting Politics and the London Missionary Society in 1830s Britain," *Journal of Church and State* 48.2 (2006): 379–398; James E. Bradeley, *Religion, Revolution and English Radicalism: Non-conformity in Eighteenth-Century Politics and Society* (Cambridge: Cambridge University Press, 1990); Michael R. Watts, *The Dissenters: Volume II The Expansion of Evangelical*

INTRODUCTION

response, ministers including Kinghorn brought petitions to protest against it.[12] On the social scale, mobs insulted and attacked dissenting ministers for their Whiggism and attitudes toward the Revolutions.[13] Questions were raised, even among the Dissenters, regarding their relationship with the Puritans, and as Baptist minister Richard Hutchings (d. 1804) pointed out, the rational Dissenters were from the illegitimate line as they abandoned "their traditional Calvinism, both as a set of doctrines and as an ascetic moral code."[14] The influence of rationalism was immense, as by the end of the eighteenth cen-

Nonconformity (Oxford: Clarendon Press, 1995), 347-452. Also see Antonia Fraser, *The King and the Catholics: England, Ireland, and the Fight for Religious Freedom, 1780-1829* (New York: Nan A. Talese/Doubleday, 2018).

[12] See Wolever, ed., *The Life and Works of Joseph Kinghorn*, I, 339-341.

[13] The most infamous attack was the Priestley Riots or the Birmingham Riots of 1791 (July 14-17). As the mob attacked Joseph Priestley and burned down his church and house, the famous Socinian Dissenter migrated to the United States. Other instances include the Woodstock Riot (1794), in which Baptist minister James Hinton was attacked (see Michael A.G. Haykin, *"Accounted Worthy to Bear in My Body the Marks of the Lord Jesus": James Hinton, the Persecution of English Dissent, and the Woodstock Riot* [Louisville, KY: The Andrew Fuller Center for Baptist Studies, 2018]; on the account of the riot, see Haykin, *"Accounted Worthy to Bear in My Body the Marks of the Lord Jesus"*, 25 n61); and the Aylsham riot (1808), in which on a Sunday evening local mobs "behaved in a very disorderly manner in the chapel, and carried off the minister by force to the Dog Inn" (Charles Mackie, *Norfolk Annals: A Chronological Record of Remarkable Events in the Nineteenth Century 1801-1805* [Norwich: Office of the Norfolk Chronicle, 1901], I, 74).

[14] John Seed, *Dissenting Histories: Religious Division and the Politics of Memory in Eighteenth-Century England* (Edinburgh: Edinburgh University Press, 2008), 131. See Richard Hutchings, *Gospel Truths Displayed, and Gospel Ministers Duty, in a Day of Great Defection Proved, in a Sermon Preached Before the Society of Protestant Dissenters, Meeting at the New-York Coffee-House: Occasioned by the Rejection of the Dissenters Bill. Delivered at the Rev. Mr. Dowars' Meeting-House, in Little Ayliffe-Street, Goodman's-Fields, April 13, 1773. With an Address to the Orthodox Party Who Joined in the Late Application* (London, 1773).

tury, English Presbyterians were completely given over to Socinianism.[15] The impact was not merely theological. Existentially, as "communities of memory," one's "continuing loyalty to Dissent was a commitment to a founding historical moment—a commitment that needed renewing."[16]

Meanwhile, when the Evangelical Revival led by George Whitefield (1714-1770), John Wesley (1703-1791), and Howell Harris (1714-1773) occurred in the early 1700s, "the British movement and its expression in England, *ab initio*, mainly occurred outside the ranks of Dissent."[17] Congregationalists like Isaac Watts (1674-1748) and Philip Doddridge (1702-1751) were the first among the Dissenters to welcome the revival.[18]

---

[15] On the Rational Dissent, see George H. Williams, "Socinianism and Deism: From Eschatological Elitism to Universal Immortality?," *Historical Reflections/Réflexions Historiques* 2.2 (1976): 265-290; R. K. Webb, "The Emergence of Rational Dissent," in *Enlightenment and Religion: Rational Dissent in Eighteenth-Century Britain*, edited by Knud Haakonssen (Cambridge: Cambridge University Press, 1996), 12-41; Daniel L. Wykes, "The Contribution of the Dissenting Academy to the Emergence of Rational Dissent," in *Enlightenment and Religion*, edited by Haakonssen, 99-139; A. M. C. Waterman, "The Nexus Between Theology and Political Doctrine in Church and Dissent," in *Enlightenment and Religion*, edited by Haakonssen, 193-218; Alan Tapper, "Priestley on Politics, Progress and Moral Theology," in *Enlightenment and Religion*, edited by Haakonssen, 272-286; R. K. Webb, "Rational Piety," in *Enlightenment and Religion*, edited by Haakonssen, 287-311; Maurice Wiles, *Archetypal Heresy: Arianism through the Centuries* (Oxford: Clarendon, 1996); John Redwood, *Reason, Ridicule and Religion: The Age of Enlightenment in England 1660-1750* (Cambridge, MA: Harvard University Press, 1976); Sarah Mortimer, *Reason and Religion in the English Revolution: The Challenge of Socinianism* (Cambridge: Cambridge University Press, 2010).

[16] Seed, *Dissenting Histories*, 132.

[17] R. Philip Roberts, *Continuity and Change: London Calvinistic Baptists and the Evangelical Revival 1760-1820* (Wheaton, IL: Richard Owen Roberts, 1989), 46. W. R. Ward traced the trans-Atlantic movement to its continental origin, see Ward, *The Protestant Evangelical Awakening* (Cambridge: Cambridge University Press, 1992).

[18] On Watts and evangelicalism, see Graham Beynon, *Isaac Watts: Reason, Passion and the Revival of Religion* (London; New York: Bloomsbury, 2016); On Doddridge and evangelicalism, Robert Strivens, *Philip Doddridge and the Shaping of Evangelical Dissent* (London; New York: Routledge, 2016).

INTRODUCTION

Baptists, in general, were not imparted by the revival until the 1770s and 1780s, though they claimed the influence of Jonathan Edwards (1703-1758) upon their change.[19] Since Samuel Johnson (1709-1784) defined the word "evangelical" as "Agreeable to gospel; consonant to the Christian law revealed in the holy gospel; contained in the gospel," W. R. Ward (1925-2010) pointed out that the word was used synonymously to mean "renewal and improvement."[20] Thus, the Evangelical Revival diminished (or at least weakened) the Conformity-vs-Nonconformity division. Instead, it drew lines between "evangelical" (or ardent) and nominal Christians. Consequently, evangelical-piety-based catholicity could be achieved in a divided religious world.[21] Baptists once again found themselves in an existential crisis, as debates over the sacraments and church membership were rekindled. At the core, questions were raised over the Baptist identity and their relationship with

---

[19] On how London Baptists welcomed the Evangelical Revival, see Roberts, *Continuity and Change*, 87-162. Also see Anthony Cross, *Useful Learning: Neglected Means of Grace in the Reception of the Evangelical Revival among English Particular Baptists* (Eugene, OR: Pickwick, 2017). Also see Michael A. G. Haykin, "Great Admirers of the Transatlantic Divinity: Some Chapters in the Story of Baptist Edwardsianism," in *After Jonathan Edwards: The Courses of the New England Theology*, edited by Oliver D. Crisp and Douglas A. Sweeney (Oxford: Oxford University Press, 2012), 197-207; Peter J. Morden, *Offering Christ to the World: Andrew Fuller (1754-1815) and the Revival of Eighteenth Century Particular Baptist Life* (Bletchley, Milton Keynes: Paternoster, 2003).

[20] Samuel Johnson, "Evangelical," in *A Dictionary of the English Language: In Which the Words are Deduced from Their Originals, and Illustrated in Their Different Significations by Examples from the Best Writers. To Which are Prefixed, a History of the Language and an English Grammar* (London, 1832), I, 646-647. Ward, *The Protestant Evangelical Awakening*, 345.

[21] See Roger H. Martin, *Evangelicals United: Ecumenical Stirrings in Pre-Victorian Britain, 1795-1830* (Metuchen, NJ; London: Scarecrow, 1983).

evangelical Paedobaptists. Significantly, the Communion Controversy took place soon after the formation of the Baptist Union (1813).[22]

"I Rest Your Loving Father"[23]

Though it was not uncommon to have both father and son serve as Baptist ministers in the long eighteenth century (c. 1689-1834), David and Joseph were unique in many respects. For John Ryland, Jr. (1753-1825), due to his father John Collett Ryland's (1723-1792) wild character, he was blessed to have the Anglican minister John Newton (1725-1807) as his spiritual father and mentor.[24] Unlike Hugh (1712-1781) and Caleb Evans (1737-1791), or Robert Hall, Sr. (1728-1791) and Jr. who left little for us to imagine early Baptist parenthood, the geographical distance between David and Joseph, created by their ministerial services and their diligent correspondence, providentially reserved the dots for us to link.

David Kinghorn was born on October 3, 1737, possibly at Hexham, Northumberland, to Scottish Presbyterian parents George (b. 1705) and Mary (b. 1707) Kinghorn.[25] Two days after his birth, David Kinghorn was baptized at Castle Garth

---

[22] See Ernest A. Payne, *The Baptist Union: A Short History* (London: Carey Kingsgate, 1958). It's interesting that "in 1832 the Union was re-organized and its objects were redefined. It was then felt sufficient to describe it as a union of Baptist ministers and churches 'who agree in the sentiments usually denominated evangelical'" (Payne, *The Baptist Union*, 3-4).

[23] D/KIN 2/1780 no. 130, DK to JK, January 5, 1780, Kinghorn Papers (Angus Library and Archive, Regent's Park College, Oxford). A transcription of this letter can also be found in Wilkin's biography, see Wolever, ed., *The Life and Works of Joseph Kinghorn*, I, 27.

[24] See Grant Gordon, ed., *Wise Counsel: John Newton's Letters to John Ryland, Jr.* (Edinburgh: Banner of Truth Trust, 2009).

[25] Wolever, ed., *The Life and Works of Joseph Kinghorn*, I, 7. George and Mary married on March 29, 1737, and they had at least three other children: John

INTRODUCTION

Presbyterian Church in Newcastle-upon-Tyne. David later moved to Newcastle-upon-Tyne and married Jane Andrew (d. 1763) in 1762. Jane gave birth to George on September 17, 1763, but neither the mother nor the son survived long, as Jane died a week after with postpartum infections and George only survived nine months.[26] Two years later, the again-single David met Elizabeth Jopling (1737/8–1810), who was the second daughter of Joseph Jopling of Satley.[27] In his proposing letter, Kinghorn wrote with anxiety, fearing that Elizabeth "will not thereby be offended, nor blame me for being too shy, or on the other hand, think I have had little value for my former wife, (which my conscience upbraids me for the contrary) as to think so soon of another."[28] Betty—as David addressed her—accepted the proposal. The couple then got married on April 22, 1765 at Gateshead-on-Tyne, south of Newcastle-upon-Tyne, across the river.

It was also around this time that Kinghorn began to seriously consider credobaptism and the gospel ministry—possibly due to his wife's influence.[29] With earnest prayer and diligent study, Kinghorn was finally convinced that only believers are suitable for baptism. After being baptised a second time as

---

(b. 1730; who married Elizabeth Garret [b. 1733] with son William [b. 1769]); George (b. 1732); Ann (b. 1734). For an extensive biographical sketch of David Kinghorn, see Baiyu Andrew Song, "David Kinghorn (1737–1822)," in *The British Particular Baptists*, edited by Michael A.G. Haykin and Terry Wolever (Springfield, MO: Particular Baptist Press, 2020), 5:153–174.

[26] Wolever, ed., *The Life and Works of Joseph Kinghorn*, I, 7.

[27] On the Jopling family (as well as their relationship to Henry Angus), see David Douglas, *History of the Baptist Churches in the North of England, from 1648 to 1845* (London: Houlston and Stoneman; Newcastle: Finlay and Charlton, and Pringle; Edinburgh: William Innes, 1846), 13–29; Wolever, ed., *The Life and Works of Joseph Kinghorn*, I, 7–9.

[28] David Kinghorn to Elizabeth Jopling, in Wolever, ed., *The Life and Works of Joseph Kinghorn*, I, 10.

[29] See, Kinghorn, "A Brief Account of my Call to the [ministry]," n.p.

a believer—possibly by David Fernie (1730-1789?), who was the pastor at Hexham—he became a member of the Baptist church at Tuthill-Stairs, Newcastle-upon-Tyne, where Elizabeth's cousin William Angus was also a deacon.[30]

On January 17, 1766, Joseph Kinghorn was added to the household, being the only child of the family.[31] Eight months later, David Kinghorn the shoemaker preached his first sermon at a Christian sister's house on August 8, 1766. Though a number of brethren confirmed his gifts and encouraged him to consecrate his life for the gospel ministry, David struggled with such a high calling. Like how he came to the credobaptist conviction, it was only by meditation (especially on 2 Thess. 3:5) and prayer that David was convinced in October 1767 that unless he responded to his calling with humility, he was "robbing" God.[32] Kinghorn fulfilled his calling and served as an assistant pastor at Tuthill-Stairs until 1771.[33]

In 1770, David received an invitation from the Baptist church in Bishop Burton, Yorkshire "to preach there, with a

---

[30] In a letter (July 6, 1765) to Robert Carmichael (d. 1774), minister of a small Independent church in Edinburgh, John Gill (1697-1771) recommended Fernie to fill in the former's pulpit, as he is "a man of great evangelical light, and good knowledge of the the constitution and order of churches...I direct my letters always to him—for I have had a correspondence with him for many years..." (As quoted in Douglas, *History of the Baptist Churches in the North of England*, 190). On Fernie, see Anonymous, "Tuthill-Stairs, Newcastle-upon-Tyne, Northumberland," *The Baptist Reporter, and Missionary Intelligencer* 5 (August 1848): 302-304; Douglas, *History of the Baptist Churches in the North of England*, 164-198; Allen B. Hinds, *A History of Northumberland, Volume III, Hexhamshire: Part I* (Newcastle-upon-Tyne: Andrew Reid; London: Simpkin, Marshall, Hamilton, Kent, 1896), 205-209.

[31] Though Elizabeth also gave birth to David Kinghorn, Jr., the child died at a young age. See Wolever, ed., *The Life and Works of Joseph Kinghorn*, I, 12.

[32] D/KIN 1/4 DK's statements of faith [?1770], Kinghorn Papers (Angus Library and Archive, Regent's Park College, Oxford).

[33] Wolever, ed., *The Life and Works of Joseph Kinghorn*, I, 13.

INTRODUCTION

view to the pastoral office."[34] After accepting such a call, Kinghorn arrived at Bishop Burton on May 4, 1770, and Elizabeth and Joseph later joined him on June 14.[35] A year later, Kinghorn was recognised as the pastor of the Bishop Burton congregation, and his ordination took place on May 1, 1771.[36] "With

---

[34] Wolever, ed., *The Life and Works of Joseph Kinghorn*, I, 16.

[35] Wilkin recorded an account of Elizabeth Kinghorn's journey to Bishop Burton in a letter written to one of her friends, "I like the place very well, and the people, and let me not forget to tell you that my husband had never such good health since I knew him, and is much fresher coloured of his face; Joseph [then 4 years old] thrives very well, and grows till you would scarce know him, he will be nothing but a farmer, he is so busy every day with loading corn, and one thing or another, till he goes as weary to bed as a little thresher, but whenever he meets with a little offence, he is for coming back to Newcastle again. Dear friend, we are very comfortably situated as to the world; my life was far happier than when I was at Newcastle, as the Lord is pleased to bless our family with health, which is the greatest blessing we can enjoy in this life: oh! may we walk worthy of this, and every other mercy we enjoy." Wolever, ed., *The Life and Works of Joseph Kinghorn*, I, 18-19.

[36] Wilkin records that "The service was commenced by Mr. Richard Hopper, of Nottingham, who formerly preached at Bishop Burton. He read, 1 Tim. iii, 2 Tim. ii, and Heb. xiii, prayed, and gave a short introductory discourse. Then Mr. William Crabtree [1720-1811], of Bradford, asked some questions, 1st, of the people, 2nd, of Mr. Kinghorn, who thereupon gave his confession of faith, after which Mr. [Joseph] Gawkrodger [1715-1798], of Bridlington, offered prayer, with *imposition of hands*, and Mr. Crabtree preached from 1 Cor. iv, 2. The whole service lasted from a quarter-past ten till half-past two: four hours and a quarter! but still the good friends were not satisfied: for at four they assembled again, when Mr. Gawkrodger preached from Eph. v, 2, after which three deacons were ordained by prayer and laying on of hands." Wolever, ed., *The Life and Works of Joseph Kinghorn*, I, 19.

On William Crabtree, see Isaac Mann, *Memoirs of the Late Rev. Wm. Crabtree, First Pastor of the Baptist Church at Bradford, Yorkshire: To Which is added a Sermon, Preached to the Church at the Ordination of the Rev. Joshua Wood, of Halifax, August 6, 1760* (London, 1815); Henry Dowson, *The Centenary: A History of the First Baptist Church, Bradford, from its commencement in 1753...* (Leeds: J. Heaton & Son; London: Houlston & Stoneman; Bradford: Woodhead & Worsnop, 1854).

An interesting note about Gawkrodger can be found in David and Joseph's correspondence in 1794, regarding the then 79-year-old Gawkrodger's marriage to Mrs. Tettle, widow of the late Mr. Thomas Tettle of Hunmanby (Wolever, ed., *The Life and Works of Joseph Kinghorn*, I, 236-237).

PUBLIC WORSHIP

honour and success," Kinghorn preached the gospel tirelessly to his congregation, and in his twenty-nine-year ministry, over thirty persons were baptised and joined the church.[37] However, in 1799, over the issue of church discipline, David Kinghorn and the congregation found themselves in irreconcilable disagreements, and by the end of that year, Kinghorn was dismissed and moved to Norwich.

"Yours in Duty and Affection"
While enjoyed his childhood in Bishop Burton, Joseph was sent to a local grammar school on March 6, 1775. According to his biographer, at this time, Joseph learned Latin, Greek, English literature, mathematics, as well as Thomas Gurney's (1705–1770) brachygraphy.[38] In December 1779, David Kinghorn was informed that a Mr. Cliffe at Hull, "a clock and watchmaker...was willing to take Joseph, then nearly fourteen, as an apprentice."[39] After their son's relocation, David and Elizabeth expressed their concerns and love for their boy in letters. It is through reading this two-decade-long practice of letter-writing that we have a glimpse of the unique filial relationship. Unfortunately, as the aged couple removed from Bishop Burton to live with Joseph in 1799, the father-and-son correspondence ended. On January 25, 1780, David wrote

> My dear child: As I cannot have the pleasure of speaking to you as usual, I take this opportunity of expressing my sincere regard for your welfare. As I have endeavoured to give you the best advice I was capable

---
[37] Skingle, comp., *The Story of a Country Baptist Church*, 9.
[38] Wolever, ed., *The Life and Works of Joseph Kinghorn*, I, 26.
[39] Wolever, ed., *The Life and Works of Joseph Kinghorn*, I, 27.

INTRODUCTION

of, I should cease to love, if I did not continue to recommend to you a life of piety, that is, repentance toward God, and faith in our Lord Jesus Christ; together with a practical observance of the duties of religion and morality which your years and circumstances in life call for at your hand.[40]

The father continues,

Be careful, my dear son, to read the sacred scriptures when you have opportunity, and daily to pray to God to keep you from every evil, and humbly thank him for every mercy you receive from him: Above all things remember to keep holy the Lord's day. He that neglects to honour the Lord in his house or that spends the Lord's Day idlely [sic] need not wonder if God suffer him to run into all manner of sin. Oh, be careful that you do not commit little evils, for a commission of small sins (as some call them) make way for the commission of greater. Remember the words of Solomon. Prov 1:10. My son, if sinners entice thee, consent thou not. Thy mother and I seldom have thee out of our mind, but we hope that thou wilt be well used by thy master and mistress and that thou wilt be studious to please them by a constant application to business and a submissive behaviour.[41]

Interestingly, unlike many later evangelicals in the nineteenth century, Joseph Kinghorn did not have a dramatic experience of conversion. Growing up in a genuine Christian family, Joseph was deeply influenced by the teachings and examples of

---

[40] DK to JK, January 5, 1780, Kinghorn Papers.
[41] DK to JK, January 5, 1780, Kinghorn Papers.

his parents.[42] David baptised his son on Easter Sunday, April 20, 1783. A year later (August 20, 1784), Joseph was sent to Bristol to study with Caleb Evans (1737-1791), and it was there that Kinghorn met and developed friendships with Samuel Pearce (1766-1799), James Hinton (1761-1823), Anthony Robinson (1762-1827), and William Richards (1749-1818).[43] With financial support from the Baptist Education Fund, Joseph completed his training in 1788 and immediately entered ministry. From May 1788 to March 1789, Joseph preached regularly at Milton Street Baptist church at Fairford, Gloucestershire. However, due to theological differences (i.e. Antinomianism and Hyper-Calvinism), Joseph left the church and accepted a call from St. Mary's Baptist Church at Norwich on March 28,

---

[42] Joseph expressed his Christian affections as early as 1781, which was possibly a consequence of his study of the Bible. In his letter to David and Elizabeth on May 9, 1781, Joseph wrote "beautifully": "I have reason to thank God for protecting and preserving me from evil, he only can protect us and guide us in the right way. It is a great blessing when our hearts' desire is after the Lord, and then all sublunary things are felt to be in subjection to him; then we find most peace in our minds—real, not imaginary peace." (Wolever, ed., *The Life and Works of Joseph Kinghorn*, I, 31) Or in a letter to his parents on July 18, 1781 Joseph wrote, "...happy are we, happy am I, when I find the light of God's countenance; he has never deceived me in withholding his blessing: no, nor ever will, so long as I can earnestly seek him, I hope I may truly say, I have found the above true. Who then, for the perishing joys of earth, would part with the eternal joys of heaven? I hope the Lord, of his great goodness, will keep me from doing this..." (Wolever, ed., *The Life and Works of Joseph Kinghorn*, I, 32).

On evangelical conversion in general, see D. Bruce Hindmarsh, *The Evangelical Conversion Narrative: Spiritual Autobiography in Early Modern England* (Oxford: Oxford University Press, 2005); Miyon Chung, "Conversion and sanctification," in *The Cambridge Companion to Evangelical Theology*, edited by Timothy Larsen and Daniel J. Treier (Cambridge: Cambridge University Press, 2007), 109-124.

[43] On William Richards, see John Oddy, *The Writings of the Radical Welsh Baptist Minister William Richards (1749-1818)* (Lewiston, NY; Queenston, ON; Ceredigion, Wales: Edwin Mellen, 2008). Richards later became a Socinian, though he was invited to preach the sermon for the congregation at Kinghorn's ordination.

INTRODUCTION

1789.⁴⁴ On January 17, 1790, Kinghorn accepted the call, and he was received as a member on February 14, 1790. At Joseph's ordination, which took place on May 20, 1790, David Kinghorn delivered the pastoral charge from 1 Timothy 4:16.

Though the Norwich pastor was called twice to leave his pastorate for the principalship at the newly-founded Baptist academies (Northern [1804] and Stepney [1809]), Joseph turned them down with the conviction that his primary calling was that of a pastor. For forty-three years, Joseph Kinghorn faithfully laboured in the gospel ministry, particularly in preaching. As his hearers observed: "His sermons were the result primarily of his diligent and prayerful attention to the subject; and more remotely, of the immense amount of reading and study, to which he had devoted himself."⁴⁵ Martin Hood Wilkin noticed that even Edward Irving (1792-1834) was impressed by Kinghorn's "happy power of illustration."⁴⁶ Moreover, as John Bane (1790-1855), minister of the church planted by Kinghorn at Aylsham, Norfolk, stated, "What a holy unction was manifest in the devotion and fervour of his prayers, what humbling views he had of himself as a sinner before God,

---

⁴⁴ The church originally wished to call Thomas Dunn (d. 1833), who was Kinghorn's classmate at Bristol. Dunn visited and supplied the pulpit at St. Mary's after Rees David's (1749-1788) sudden death until Lady Day, March 25, 1789. According to the church minute book, Dunn suggested to call Kinghorn instead. At the time, St. Mary's had 700-800 regular attendants and 120 members. The church minute book records that Kinghorn received an invitation to stay for six months on May 10, 1789. It was agreed that Kinghorn could visit Yorkshire from May 19 to July 17, during which time Dan Williams of London supplied the pulpit. The church then decided to invite Kinghorn for pastoral charge on December 3, 1789. Special note is indicated that at this occasion woman members were allowed to vote.
⁴⁵ Wolever, ed., *The Life and Works of Joseph Kinghorn*, I, 444.
⁴⁶ Wolever, ed., *The Life and Works of Joseph Kinghorn*, I, 445.

how ardently would he pray for acceptance through the atonement of his Son..."[47]

Kinghorn clearly understood the gospel and his calling, as he stated,

> The most important enquiry that can engage our minds, relates to our spiritual state. Christianity is as *true* now, as it was the first day you felt its power; and to you it ought to be *more* important than ever, because you are nearer that world where its evidence and glory will blaze forth with inextinguishable ardour, and where it will be found a source of unspeakable and eternal joy to those who have sought its blessings. True Godliness will lead us to maintain the Christian profession, and to seek the glory of God, both in what we *do* and in what we *avoid*. This forms a part of the evidence that we are the children of God. It is consistent with every important duty in life, and will call us away from nothing, but what either in nature or in degree would prove a real evil. Let us exhort one another *daily, lest we be deceived by the deceitfulness of sin*, and in the end become *weary and faint in our minds*. May we grow in a deep, serious sense, of the importance of religion in the heart, as a *living principle!* For, even maintaining an honourable profession is not enough, if it does not proceed from that true, inward religion, and directed by his word. The fear of God, and the love of God, proceeding from faith in Jesus Christ, form the great principles of a Christian's character. *For the grace of God, that bringeth salvation, hath appeared unto all men, teaching us, that denying ungodliness and worldly lusts, we should live soberly, righteously, and godly, in this present world; looking for that*

---

[47] Wolever, ed., *The Life and Works of Joseph Kinghorn*, I, 445.

INTRODUCTION

blessed hope, and the glorious appearing of the great God and our Saviour Jesus Christ, who gave himself for us, that he might redeem us from all iniquity, and purify unto himself a peculiar people, zealous of good works." Titus 2:11-14. The comfort and edification of a Christian Society depend[s] on the influence of these sentiments in the hearts of its members, preserving them in a steady and honourable religious profession. It is the living energy of these holy principles, which constitutes the true prosperity of a Christian church. Many other things are *desirable*, but these are *essential*. Here you are all concerned, for the life of the whole is the life of every part united together. I might appeal to you, whether the serious influence of Christianity did not once produce an important effect on your hopes and on your whole character? And how much has it since tended, both in health and affliction, to promote serenity of mind, and to strengthen your faith in God? But I trust that I need not enlarged. While we make our profession together, may we remember our high calling; our day is fast spending; there are many important ways in which we are called to glorify God, which are peculiar to the present state, and which we ought therefore to consider as calling for our especial attention. May we not be *slothful, but followers of them who through faith and patience inherit the promises.* What an invaluable privilege, if at last we are found members of the church which is above; acknowledged by Jesus Christ as his brethren; as the children of God once scattered abroad, then gathered into one body, and united with *the general assembly and church of the first-born, whose names are written in heaven!*[48]

---

[48] Joseph Kinghorn, *An Address to a Friend, on Church Communion: With an Appendix, containing a Brief Statement of the Sentiments of the Baptists on the Ordinance of Baptism*, 3rd ed. (Norwich, 1824), iv-vi.

With this kind of love for truth, Kinghorn laboured tirelessly in studying. During his lifetime, he learned various languages, including Hebrew, Greek, Chaldee, Syriac, Arabic, Latin, and German. Like Andrew Fuller (1754-1815), who famously declared that "eminent spirituality in a minister is usually attended with eminent usefulness," Kinghorn understood the quintessential connection between human learning, personal piety, and public ministry.[49] As Kinghorn pointed out, students need to "cultivate that Christian character which was the first great reason why you were encouraged to turn your attention to the ministry."[50] Thus, the goal of formal theological education is the cultivation of character. Regarding the relationship between learning and piety, Kinghorn explained that "piety will neither confer learning, nor powers of reasoning acutely; but other things being equal, that man is likely to discern the will of God with the most correctness, who imbibes the largest portion of the spirit of the gospel."[51] For Kinghorn,

> Ministers should read the scriptures as *Christians*, that their own souls may be nourished by the word of life; and as the servants of the church of Christ, they should read them carefully and diligently, that they

---

[49] Andrew Fuller, *The Qualifications and Encouragement of a Faithful Minister Illustrated by the Character and Success of Barnabas*, in *The Complete Works of the Rev. Andrew Fuller: With a Memoir of His Life, by Andrew Gunton Fuller*, edited by Joseph Belcher (Reprint, Harrisonburg, VA: Sprinkle, 1988), I, 143.

[50] Joseph Kinghorn, *Practical Cautions to Students and Young Ministers. The Substance of a Sermon Preached at Bradford, in the County of York; At the Annual Meeting of the Northern Baptist Education Society, August 27, 1817* (Norwich, 1817), 8-9.

[51] Joseph Kinghorn, *Advice and Encouragement to Young Ministers. Two Sermons, Addressed Principally to the Students of the Two Baptist Academies, at Stepney and at Bristol. The First Preached June 23, 1814, at the Rev. Dr. Rippon's Meeting, Carter-lane, Southwark; The Second, August 3, 1814, at the Rev. Dr. Ryland's. Broad Mead, Bristol* (Norwich, 1814), 38.

may learn the truth in its simplicity, and have it engraven on their hearts, in the words taught by the Holy Ghost. It is an important thing to have a taste for the language and representations of the Bible, so that the faith which we profess, may be the evident impression of the words of inspiration; and the track of our thought, be the same with that in the sacred volume.[52]

To reach this goal, ministers are told to read the scriptures "in their original language," and in so doing, to "depend on no man's learning and authority, but go to the fountain head of the stream, which makes glad the city of our God."[53] Kinghorn believed that reading the scriptures in the original languages can illuminate the mind, and that it is advantageous to read "the displays of the glory of God as he himself made them known, and of beholding them without a veil."[54] He continued, "we behold them stript of the garment in which modern expression [i.e., translations] has clothed them, and standing in that native simplicity, in which they were first exhibited by *holy men of old, who spake as they were moved by the Holy Ghost.*"[55] With his learning, Kinghorn earned the reputation that "in his own denomination he was inferior only to Dr. [John] Gill [1697-1771] in an intimate acquaintance with Rabbinical literature."[56]

Besides his domestic ministry and studies, Kinghorn was also actively involved in the Baptist Missionary Society (including his two expeditions to Scotland on behalf of the BMS in 1818 and 1822), London Society for Promoting Christianity

---

[52] Kinghorn, *Advice and Encouragement to Young Ministers*, 8-9.
[53] Kinghorn, *Advice and Encouragement to Young Ministers*, 10.
[54] Joseph Kinghorn, *Advice and Encouragement to Young Ministers*, 10.
[55] Kinghorn, *Advice and Encouragement to Young Ministers*, 10.
[56] Wolever, ed., *The Life and Works of Joseph Kinghorn*, I, 449.

among Jews (two of his sermons at the Jewish chapel in London were printed), as well as in local church plantings. He was also a member of the Norwich Speculative Society, where he defended the Christian faith and presented the gospel to local intellectuals. As an apologist, Kinghorn defended Christian orthodoxy—in particular, the doctrine of the Trinity and the divinity of Christ—as well as Baptist ecclesiology. Being a faithful and useful servant of God, Kinghorn "fit to live, was greatly fit to die!"[57]

---

[57]Amelia Alderson Opie (1769-1853), "'Lines' on Hearing it said continually, that our late Revered friend, J. Kinghorn, was 'fit to die'," in Cecilia Lucy Brightwell, *Memoir of Amelia Opie* (London: The Religious Tract Society, 1855), 99; also see Wolever, ed., *The Life and Works of Joseph Kinghorn*, I, 457.

PUBLIC WORSHIP

Considered and Enforced,

BY

JOSEPH KINGHORN.

"NOT FORSAKING THE ASSEMBLING OF OURSELVES TOGETHER AS THE MANNER OF SOME IS."

Hebrews X. 25.

Norwich:

PRINTED AND SOLD BY

R. BACON, No. 12, COCKEY-LANE;

And may be had of J. Annis, London-Lane; and of W. Button, No. 24, Paternoster-Row, London.

1800.

PRICE SIX-PENCE.

Original Preface

No apology can be made for offering the following pages to the public eye, but the importance of the subject, and the motive of the author. He confesses the superior talents of preceding writers, and does not mean at all to undervalue their works, but only to add a small attempt to forward the good cause in which they have laboured. He is aware many more observations might have been made, and the subject placed in additional points of light. But he wished not to write a book but only a pamphlet, and indeed a small pamphlet, that it might have the chance of circulating and being read, where anything large on the subject could not make its way. The lower as well as the higher classes need exhortation and encouragement to attend to public worship. Some it is true in all stations from age, infirmity, or other reasons, may be either totally or considerably freed from the obligation that lies on those who have health and opportunity. But such cases are easily discernible; we are to apt to make the most of the excuses in our power, and more often need exhortations to activity, than the contrary. It deserves enquiry, what tendency the relaxed sentiments and practice of the present age respecting public worship have had on those who have fairly felt their influence; what is the most likely way of preserving the present professors of Christianity from the fatal effects of indifference and infidelity;[1] and how we shall best keep

---

[1] The word "professor" means a person publicly declares convictions. For instance, in Samuel Johnson's dictionary, an artist is defined as "professor of an

the rising generation from that early opposition to all religion of which we have seen too many instances. We cannot expect that every endeavour will be successful, but nothing can be hoped for if nothing be attempted. From a proper regard to God's worship some good effects will follow. And the more we combine with it, a conscientious and wise attention to the other parts of religion, the greater will be the force of our example and the prevalence of our prayers. The remarks here before our reader are left to his serious consideration; May the blessing of God follow whatever is agreeable to his will!

---

art," or a lawyer, "a professor of law." Accordingly, a Christian, in the eighteenth century, means "a professor of the religion of Christ." (Samuel Johnson, *A Dictionary of the English Language: In Which the Words are deduced from their Originals, Explained in their Different Meanings, and Authorized by the Names of the Writers in whose Works they are found...* (3rd ed., Dublin, 1768).

"Infidelity" means "want of faith;" "disbelief of Christianity;" or "treachery; deceit; breach of contract or trust."

1
A Creature's Duty

The first consideration I would exhibit is, that public worship is one of God's appointed ways of receiving the homage of his creatures.

The importance of Christians assembling themselves together for the worship of God, has been very generally acknowledged; and those who have argued against the practice have seldom made much impression, except on such as only wanted an apology to neglect it.

Very few, who pay any regard to religion, will seriously say, they do not believe it is the duty of men publicly to worship God; and those few are not the objects of the present address.[1] I would wish to set before the professors of Christianity some considerations on this subject, not so much to convince them of its propriety, as to put them in remembrance of what may excite an earnest and steady regard to an important duty.

Without going back to the very early ages of the world, and calling in the aid either of conjecture or criticism to assist us in the enquiry how men worshipped God before the days of Noah or Abraham, it will be enough for our present purpose to observe, that as soon as God gave to men an extensive revelation of his will, public worship immediately appeared to be of high consequence. I think there are traces that a day separated to the service of God must have been known, and public worship probably in use earlier than the giving of the Law to Israel by

---

[1] "Religion" means "virtue as founded upon reverence of God, and expectation of future rewards and punishments;" or "a system of divine faith and worship as opposite to others."

Moses; but at that time at least, a day of worship was specified and guarded by awful sanctions. A tabernacle for worship was ordered to be erected; regulations concerning it were given; three times a year all the males were ordered to appear before the Lord, though the place of their residence might be very far distant; and national festivals were connected with religious services, in which all those who were, or who in the course of time would be heads of families in Israel, were expected to be present to pay their homage to their God.

The Jewish Sabbath was separated from other days for the purposes of rest and religion. It referred to the creation, when God *rested* the seventh day and *hallowed* it (Exodus 22:9, 10, 11), and to the deliverance of the children of Israel from Egypt, and event of great importance in their religious services (Deuteronomy 5:14, 15). It was on the Sabbath days, both those which regularly came every week and some other days of special appointment, that the most solemn of their sacred rites were performed; and it was a singular Law, that on these days *no servile work* was to be done. The meanest servant in every family enjoyed a day of *rest*. And while *labour* was forbidden and an attention to *religion* commanded and encouraged, did it not as far as was consistent with any liberty of action, call upon the people to worship their God on his Sabbath, and if even they were far distant from his tabernacle, to spend the day in a manner not inconsistent with its institution?

At the time of Jesus Christ, we find the public worship of God attended to in some cases even with a superstitious regard. Besides the temple worship which was at Jerusalem, after the captivity the worship of the synagogue was instituted in many parts of the country, where prayers were offered to God, and his word was read to the people every Sabbath day.

Consideration I

To this practice our Lord gave the sanction of his attendance and assistance (Luke 4:16). And after he ascended, not only did the apostles assemble with the Jews to converse with them in their synagogues (Acts 17:2), but they collected Christians into bodies, who met on the first day of the week to worship God by prayer and praise, to read his word or exhort each other to attend to it (Acts 11:42; 22:7; 1 Corinthians 16:2; 1 Timothy 2:1; Hebrews 10:25; Colossians 3:16, etc.).

Thus, the practice of worshipping God, as a token of our dependence and gratitude, has lived through various ages—He has changed the dispensation of Moses for that of Christ; he has abolished the day and the rituals of his former service; he has called now the Gentiles of different nations to know his name; he has excluded his ancient people from their privileges, and has made strangers partakers of his favour—but still through all these changes, the obligation to attend to his worship is evidently considered as abiding in force.

Shall the professors of the religion of Jesus be indisposed to "ascribe to the Lord the glory due his name" (Psalm 29:2)? Have not they above all men who ever lived, reasons for gratitude and praise? Are not they peculiarly recipients of God's favour, dependants on his manifold grace? And shall they be averse to render unto God the homage he has ever claimed, and which through all ages good men have ever given? Where is our similarity in character to those who have gone before us, if when our brethren say, "Let us go to the house of the Lord" (Psalm 122:1)—we turn aside and cry, "What a weariness this is" (Malachi 1:13)?

2
Knowing God
& Ourselves

The public worship of God has a great tendency to keep up in our minds, a sense of his character and of our situation.

Every part of it suggests that God is great and that we should be lowly before him; that he is holy, but that we are full of sin and imperfection; that he is the great fountain of all good and that we are dependent on him for the blessings of providence and the more important blessings of grace. At all times these things are acknowledged. They are the first principles of true religion. From which of them can we withhold our assent? Which of them ought we not daily to feel and acknowledge? How often has even the presence of our fellow Christians impressed us with a sense of God's greatness and condescension and of our own unworthiness in his sight? When we have recollected that our adorations were in company with those of others, who perhaps bowed at the divine throne with a deeper humility—that our praises were joined with those of others, who perhaps felt more gratitude than we—that our petitions for mercies were the same as those of others, who might pray with more earnestness or more faith than ourselves—that God knows every character and lets not even a sigh escape his notice, and that we altogether—the largest assembly of worshippers that could be found either in earth or heaven—the whole universe itself and all therein are nothing before him—how much have these thoughts tended to fill our minds with a sense of his glory!

> Who in the skies can be compared to the Lord? Who among the sons of might is like the Lord, a God greatly to be feared in the council of the holy ones, and awesome above all who are around him? (Psalm 89:6-7);

> For thus says the One who is high and lifted up, who inhabits eternity, whose name is Holy: "I dwell in the high and holy place, and also with him who is of a contrite and lowly spirit, to revive the spirit of the lowly, and to revive the heart of the contrite" (Isaiah 57:15).

Nothing is more calculated to fix any sentiment deeply in the mind than publicly and frequently joining with others to express it. By this means what might otherwise have been neglected is often impressed as a principle of action never to be forgotten. A man feels his heart attached to the truth which he is habitually declaring. It becomes necessary that he who has been accustomed publicly to worship his maker should again go and offer to him his praises and his prayers. He has confessed so often he is dependent on him for all things, and lives by his mercy, that the impression follows him and urges him to go on in the path of duty. He asks (and there is reason in the enquiry): Do I not still need, as much as ever, the blessings of grace? Has not God a right to every just acknowledgement I can make of his character? Why should I then be so averse to express what I cannot but feel? And why not express it where I have been taught to feel it, "in the company of the upright, in the congregation" (Psalm 111:1)?

It will be objected by some, we feel so little elevation of soul in the worship of God that we scarce can think it worth our

Consideration II

attention. But let me plainly ask: Do you wish to have a sense of God's character live in your minds? Do you cultivate the means of promoting it? If not, it is no wonder that the worship of God gives you little pleasure. He who wishes to forget his God, let him keep away from it; he acts consistently. He who will only attend upon it while his passions can be excited by something that shall surprise by its novelty, and who absents himself when he becomes familiarised to what it exhibits, is not acting on the call of duty, but on a principle which he probably little suspects; he is laying more stress on having his mind pleased than rendered obedient. If the above objection be made by those who do wish habitually to keep in view the character of their God, let me ask them what they are likely to gain by absence from his worship? Is it probable he will be more upon their minds, when they are not called to reflect on him, than when they are? Surely here the observation of every Christian will be on my side. Cold and heartless as our devotion has frequently been, we should often not have thought upon God, had it not been for his worship. And how many times has it happened, that while thus employed, our hearts have been impressed in a manner we have little expected, and we have said with the disciples on another occasion, "it is good that we are here" (Matthew 17:4; Mark 9:5; Luke 9:33).

And shall we encourage our indolence by neglecting what has been the means of so much utility, and may still be of very important consequence? Have we yet to learn the value of an habitual disposition to worship the Lord? Is there no pleasure—no profit in devotion but when the mind is stretched by representations which surprise, and the imagination is fired by the sublime? Are we in no danger of forgetting God? Have we no need of being reminded of our situation and of his greatness and goodness? Is there no reason to fear lest indifference should steal into the mind? Were these things properly to impress us, the most distant thought of trifling with our duty would be vanished far away.

3
A Means of Witness

The public worship of God is an important means of promoting religious knowledge.

A course of religious instruction has been joined more closely with the worship of God since the coming of Christ, than it was before; and it is a direct consequence of his plan. He said, "My kingdom is not of this world" (John 18:36). It is a kingdom supported by the effects of instruction, by men who having learned of Jesus are not regulated by worldly maxims. Now where can the instruction Christianity furnishes be more conveniently given than in connection with the worship it enjoins? Real Christians are men and women distinguished by their having imbibed the doctrine and spirit of their divine master; and from the weakness of their powers and the imperfections of their characters they find there is always something to learn and something to amend. Hence the practice begun in the days of the apostles has ever been found both wise and necessary, to join to the worship of God some attention to his holy word.

Here we might appeal to our own experience and observation. Almost all who make the concerns of their souls and the knowledge of the will of God serious objects, owe much to the instruction joined with worship. By this many of them were first let to the enquiry, "what must I do to be saved?" (Acts 16:30); by this it was promoted. One ray of light succeeded another. The importance of eternity—the worth of the soul—the lost and helpless situation of man in the presence of his God—

PUBLIC WORSHIP

and the way of salvation by faith in a crucified Saviour, engage the attention. They saw these things as true—they felt them as important—they sought unto God through Jesus Christ for mercy, and they found that true religion was a vast system, which had much to present to the understanding, and much to animate the heart. The Bible was then valued as containing the only pure description of God's will and of the way to eternal life, and was on this account read with earnest diligence. Whatever was calculated to explain or enforce any part of it was heard with pleasure. Hence arose a motive to frequent the worship of God unknown before. Difference of situation may have made us more or less indebted to it, but in general we all have reason to value it; it gave us ideas, guided our reasonings, directed us to new views of the sacred scriptures, and communicated much information which otherwise we should not have obtained.

Perhaps it will be said, though this was once a reason for attending on religious worship, yet now we have obtained from it the principal information it has to bestow—its end is answered. This is not true. Religious worship is of great importance, even if it produced no additional information; but it is impossible for any man to say, he shall obtain from it no more. We had in everything, that we forget what was once most familiar, which we have not been for a time in the habit of attention to it. It is the same in religion as in other things, forgetfulness follows inattention. And what is forgetfulness, but the road back again to ignorance? By continued attendance this would be prevented. Farther, it is impossible to listen to just descriptions of religion without increasing our knowledge. We think of it when otherwise we should not; it appears to the mind in various light: its different parts are often in view; its serious

Consideration III

importance forwards enquiry by an appeal to the heart; and by the whole, "the man of God" is perfected, "equipped for every good work" (2 Timothy 3:17).

Here it will be objected, that this supposes the only means of information is public instruction; but with our Bible, and other good books to assist us, can we not make as much progress at home as in a place of worship? The subjects of religion are often treated with less ability from the pulpit than in the writings of good men which we can consult. To wave other answers to this objection for the present, let us come to plain fact.

Do those who reason in this manner, and neglect convenient opportunities of attending public worship, *actually* employ their diligence in increasing their knowledge of God's will and word? Do they not loiter away the time appropriated to the worship of God rather than improve it? Is not the objection rather an excuse for staying at home, than a description of their employment there? I leave this appeal to their consciences, let everyone answer it faithfully.

Again, another class of people often owe much to public worship, *viz.* servants and those who labour for their bread so many hours in the day as to have very little time left for cultivating their minds. These all have souls which will live for ever and be either saved or lost: But they are in situations very unfavourable to the acquisition of knowledge. Women servants, and the wives of men in the lower states of life especially, are much excluded from opportunities of improvement. How many families also are there where the fear of God is not to be found? How many—where there is a great decency and respectability of conduct, and yet no serious sense of the vast importance of godliness—nothing that would forward an enquiry into the concerns of the soul, or promote an increase of Christian knowledge? And yet numbers in such situations may, from one motive or another, be led to public worship, either occasionally or statedly. The house of God is the only place where there is a probability of their becoming acquainted with their true condition and the way to eternal life. If they are happily impressed with a sense of the importance of seeking for salvation, perhaps they have no religious acquaintance, who knows what the state of the mind is, when it labours under a sense of guilt, and has little knowledge of God's grace, and who could drop a word in season to the weary, and direct and encourage them in the good ways of God. Of what importance is the public worship of God to such persons? It is the only thing at all likely to touch their case, and afford them the information, encouragement, and exhortation they need. Hence the high value they often set upon it; and the importance of ministers keeping in mind the cases of those who more depend on them for their religious instruction than at first sight may seem probable. And here we may just add, that those Christians who need not themselves be taught the first principles of the doctrine of Christ ought not to forget, that it is in the highest degree reasonable not only to endeavour to promote their farther improvement, but also to instruct the ignorant; and that they will not in the end be losers, by any proper means of fitting others for immortality.

Farther, the rising generation frequently owe much to the instruction joined with public worship, by being accustomed to it from early life they insensibly learn something of its end and importance, something of the greatness and goodness of God, of the nature of his gospel and the obligations of men. Conscience is assisted by the habit, and they are not so easily led to

Consideration III

a complete departure from everything that is good as otherwise they might be. But besides the general impression, that religion is an affair of consequence, and that it is only the ungodly who cast it off; besides the valuable influence of habit, which often has a great ascendancy afterwards, we are not always able to estimate how much deeper many things sink into the minds of the young than we suppose. It is true at best they are but a careless set of hearers, but the constancy of a course of instruction always offers something whenever they are at all disposed to attend, and the frequent recurrence of the same or similar subjects, renders it almost certain that in time their attention will be caught by each particular part of Christianity. If ever they are the objects of address from the pulpit, and the address be made with propriety, they soon find themselves interested, and often their little countenances will fix with attention, or while they hang their heads as if they wished not to meet the eyes of any, they will acutely feel the force of what is said. A seed is sometimes planted in early life which may lie a long time before it grows up and openly produce fruit to the glory of God. And representations both of the sinful state of human nature, and of the great grace of God in his gospel may be buried many years in the memory, and in an important moment, have a resurrection—produce a valuable effect in assisting the awakened sinner to return to his God—preserve from the paths of error, and cause him with thankfulness to acknowledge the blessing, of having been early led to the house of prayer. Thus, a great deal may be done where there is little external evidence of it, in addition to the happy, I hope on the whole we may add, numerous instances of the manifest good effect of the worship of God on those who are raised up in pious families as a seed to serve God, and whose praises are sweetened by the sentiment expressed of old, he is "my father's God, and I will exalt him" (Exodus 15:2).

Are we well-wishers to the spread of religious knowledge? Are the words of Jesus the words of truth? Has he said, "No one comes to the Father except through me" (John 14:6)— "this is eternal life, that they may know you, the only true God, and Jesus Christ whom you have sent" (John 17:3)? Is there "no other name under heaven given among men by which we must be saved" (Acts 4:12)? Of what importance is it, that so public a means as the worship of God is, of spreading the knowledge of Christianity, and of exhibiting a part of its practice, should receive all the sanction that we can give it! We ought on our own accounts to be diligent in performing every Christian duty. And, ourselves apart, have we no concern for the welfare of others? Are there none who might be led by our example, or guided by our direction, to the worship of God, who otherwise might not attend to it? We stand together in society like the ears of corn in a field; when only a few are strongly moved, the motion is communicated to many more. It is not easy to say, how far the influence even of an individual may extend. Besides, are there none more nearly allied to us, to whom duty, interest, and hope should direct our attention? Can we help wishing that they may be seriously impressed with the weight of religious truth, and forward the cause of Christianity in the world? Be it then our concern to support and promote the public worship of God, and to use all prudent means of inducing others to attend it also, in hope that they may be led to *hear* and *fear* and *know* the Lord.

4
CHRISTIAN DISCIPLESHIP & COMFORT

Public worship is much connected with a Christian's moral improvement, and comfort even to the end of life.

When the apostle Paul spoke of the ends of prophesying, in 1 Corinthians 14:3 (by which he appears to intend the public instruction of the church by inspired men) he says, he that "prophesies speaks to people for their upholding and encouragement and consolation." Here though inspiration has ceased, the general ends of public worship are clearly exhibited. Good men, who have long been tutored under the sound of the gospel, often find that it still suggests what they had not before observed; thus, they are more established in the truth of the gospel, the importance of its grace, or the reality of some of its particular doctrines than they would have been. With this, a steady faith and a steady action are intimately connected. On every renewed view of the reality and excellence of the religion of Jesus, the Christian feels the motives of attention renewed also. Like a traveller who meets with a fresh assurance that his journey shall be highly prosperous, he mends his pace, and disregards the temptations to trifle or turn out of the way. This confirmation of mind in the belief of the truth, is called in Scripture being edified or build up in our most holy faith (Jude 20). Again, exhortation which is joined with worship, has often an unexpected effect. A reproof is conveyed which was neither intended nor thought of. The force of truth penetrates a good man's conscience; he sees some features of his own character, he marks the difference between them and those of Jesus his Lord; he is ashamed, he breathes out his prayer to God, and says, by his grace I will amend.

Could he be better employed? When the duties of religion are pressed on the conscience, how frequently do Christians see the obligations they are under to observe them, and the deficiencies of their past obedience, in a new or in a stronger light than before. Even an attentive mind feels the importance of being put in remembrance of what has been already learned. Many duties we should not have thought of had we not been roused by exhortation. Many of our resolutions to walk in God's ways have by the same means been most sensibly strengthened. When earnestly exhorted to attend to any plain precept, we are placed immediately in a new situation. We cannot say we know not our duty: we cannot plead ignorant of the motives of attending to it. We seem called on as in the presence of God and his people, to obey his will. We feel as if the eyes of all were upon us, and the appeal was made, whether we would regard the word of God or not.

Have these things no effect on our character? Is there ever a period when that effect is not wanted? No, while forgetfulness, imperfection, and indolence continue to mark human nature, a serious Christian never can say he needs not the language of exhortation.

Farther, comfort is another of the ends answered by divine worship. All the way through life we are exposed to difficulties and afflictions of one kind or another. The Christian takes his share of the common evils of life, from which he can plead no exemption. He has also difficulties of his own. A man who under a strong impression of the reality of another world and of

CONSIDERATION IV

the truth of the gospel, wishes to live to God, has an object in sight, which other men have not, and he has his fears as well as his hopes respecting it. He knows that to "deny himself and take up his cross and follow" Jesus Christ (Matthew 16:14; Mark 8:34; Luke 9:23) is not so easy as some may imagine. He also views the hand of God in the afflictions of life; he sees how nearly he touches on an eternal world, and the question often engages him, how shall I appear before God? He considers not afflictions as evils to be born as well as we can and shaken off as soon as we are able; he looks farther. If his affliction arises from his afflictions as evils to be born as well as we can and shaken off as soon as we are able; he looks farther. If his affliction arises from his family or friends, his concern is in part, because he views them as formed for eternity, and he is not only grieved for anything amiss in them here, but also, from the connection of both worlds, he sees the events of this life often extend their effect into that to come. If no such causes of uneasiness exist, if his afflictions arise only from disease or misfortune, still he feels a difficulty in so submitting to the hand of God, as he knows he ought. He is led to take a serious view of his life and character as in the presence of God, and feels deeply humbled on account of its various imperfections; or he may be led to say with a mind full of anxiety, "let me know why you contend against me" (Job 10:2). Perhaps too he meets with some opposition, or contempt on account of his profession of religion, so that he has nor peaceable possession of the only source of his hope. Here we see the reasons why the word of God should be displayed as suggesting consolation to the afflicted Christian in all his circumstances of sorrow. It is the glory of Christianity, that it has so much to offer to comfort those that mourn, to encourage the tempted and the feeble minded, and to sooth the Christian in his most complicated distress, by bidding him "casting all your anxieties on him," under the assurance that "he cares for you" (1 Peter 5:7).

When Christians meet for worship there are usually some in these situations. It would be very unkind were the comforts of religion never to be administered. We all in our turns need them, and know what a happy effect they often produce. "How delightful is a timely word" (Proverbs 15:23)? In all pressures of mind, we feel much support from the opinion of others. it forms a great sanction to our own. And when in the worship of God, those consolations which are drawn from God's word, and are agreeable to the experience of Christians are set before us, our minds take courage. We still feel ourselves in the society of good men, for we see they have been in similar difficulties before us. We see what is still of greater importance, that our God, great as he is, "for he knows our frame, he remembers that we are dust" (Psalm 103:14), and has provided encouragement and assistance adapted to our weakness. For these things, the worship of God is of continual importance; the experience of which often leads the Christian to say, "One thing have I asked of the Lord, that will I seek after: that I may dwell in the house of the Lord all the days of my life, to gaze upon the beauty of the Lord and to inquire in his temple" (Psalm 27:4).

5
THE CITY OF GOD REVEALED

Public worship is a central point where the professors of the religion of Christ visibly unite as his subjects, for the purpose of obeying the various parts of his will.

In the world, the righteous often are connected with the wicked; but in the worship of God, they meet in the character by which they are distinguished from the rest of mankind. It is the Church of Christ, that Christians as a body obey their Lord. They cannot keep up an attention to his ordinance of breaking bread in remembrance of him but in society. They cannot love each other as brethren, supply each other's wants, watch over and provoke each other to love and good works, without society. Their faith in the mediation and authority of one common Lord unites them together that they may reverence and obey him. This union leads them to a farther acquaintance with each other; and to an attention to those who show a wish to walk with them in the ways of God. It forms them into a body which renders the example of every individual of some consequence; gives to each a character to maintain, and places him in a situation in which he both receives the assistance of the friendship, advice, and encouragement of others, and in his turn, communicates the same advantages.

The Church of Christ is the only visible kingdom he maintains on earth, from which he daily makes his appeal to the world, and by which he carries on many of his designs of grace. But how are these ends to be answered without men unite in public worship and in an acknowledged subjection to Jesus Christ? And how feeble will be the effect if that union be not serious, vigorous, and steady? A solitary Christian may live, even as a man may live many years on a desolate island; but a Christian, steady in his worship and obedience, and upright in his conduct, lives like an active member of society; his value is daily felt; he helps forward a vast system, and assists in handing to the next generation the knowledge of eternal life! And ought he, with these views before him, to neglect his place in the house of his God, or fill it up in a careless and indifferent manner? How does he imitate his divine master in glorifying his father on earth, while he trifles away his opportunities of improvement and utility? Life is far too short, to admit much of it to be spent in indolence. Part of our day is already gone, our remaining hours are perhaps few, we must be up and doing for "night is coming, when no one can work" (John 9:4).

These things have excited a general reflection, which, before I proceed farther, I will mention; *viz.* if the ends of public worship and the characters interested therein are so many, how important the office of all those who conduct it? To pay a proper attention to the evidences of religion, that the hearers may be led to see they "did not follow cleverly devised myths" (2 Peter 1:16), to assist them in understanding their Bibles, by proper enquiries and explanations. And to keep in view at the same time both the doctrines and precepts of religion, is a very important matter. To trace the reasonings and representations of the inspired penmen and show their force, and yet to be so plain that the important truths may be apprehended and felt by the weak and ignorant. To press duty home on the conscience, and yet to deprive none of his proper share of encouragement

CONSIDERATION V

and consolation; to depress the presumptuous without crushing the humble; to be the guide of the young Christian, the assistant of the well-informed; and to support the various parts of worship in a manner that may be generally useful to those who attend, is altogether a labour which may well make us say with the apostle, "Who is sufficient for these things?" (2 Corinthians 2:16). But as man is designed by providence to be the means of doing good to his fellow man, and as a duty lies upon us all in our respective situations, it becomes us to join our endeavours and prayers, that we may encourage each other, and that our labour may not be in vain in the Lord.

And now, brethren, suffer the word of exhortation. Are the above-mentioned considerations true? How plain an inference arises from them? If even there be but a degree of truth in each, and the reader supposes the whole is somewhat overstated; still it will follow that divine worship is an important duty, and that he who would wish to improve and be useful, will consider it as one means not to be neglected. And this in reality is all that needs be granted. For he who neglects a religious duty, because there is not the strongest possible evidence concerning it, shows that he wishes to attend to as little as he can help. Who would not be ashamed of this indolence when traced to its consequences? What? The recipients of innumerable benefits—indebted to the rich grace of God for all we enjoy and all we expect—and not willing to attend to the means of glorifying God, without the obligation be marked in a way we cannot possibly resist? Is this gratitude? Is this Christian obedience? No.

Had you been the happy man who had saved a fellow creature from ruin in his business—prescribed for him medicine which had restored him from the gates of death; healed an apparently incurable breach between him and his friends; or introduced him to connections by which his happiness and interests were promoted; and besides this united him with your own family where he has great expectations—what would you think if he was remiss in attending upon you, because you had not used all the urgency and authority you might have done, in commanding him not to neglect you? And especially if attention on you was neither opposed to his duty, interest, or happiness, but only required that he should sometimes shake off an indolence of disposition? If you were not the first to complain, but from the same generosity which you had before displayed did not point to the acts of your own goodness, society would do it for you. It would become the conversation of every company, each would add his remark on the meanness of such a temper and conduct, and the whole would close in the spirit if not in the words of the prophet, when be said to Israel: "O my people, what have I done to you? How have I wearied you? Answer me!" (Micah 6:3).

If then you would be ashamed of being marked for negligence and ingratitude towards man, can you think lightly of the reasons which call on you to attend to the public worship of God? How many things in common life do you diligently pursue on far less evidence? Be *steady*, therefore, and show much you wish to promote the cause of God among men. Without this your religious example will have little weight; nor will you be the encouragement to others you might be. It has never yet appeared to be the will of God to carry on the kingdom of Christ without the union of Christians together for public worship, nor is it likely that God's plan herein should change. But if you are not steady in your attention (without some proper reasons

Consideration V

to the contrary), you are not doing what you could to assist in the support and spread of religion. Public worship could not be carried on with pleasure if some did not steadily encourage it with their presence. It is this which gives it spirit, and causes it to be attended to with advantage. But you who are negligent add nothing to either. Your conduct instead of being an encouragement to others discourages them. They feel pain and surprise at seeing what appears to them so unaccountable; for a time they form as many excuses for you as they can, even after that, they feel for what they cannot excuse—till at last weary of hoping for a change, your presence with them gives them no pleasure; your absence no pain; your example is only considered as a thing to be avoided, and you inevitably sink in the estimation of those who would have esteemed you and whom you might have benefited. Your conduct forms an excuse for the *negligent*, and this is its greatest tendency. If the cause of religion prospers, it was not your zeal that assisted it; if it sinks, you did not put forth your strength to prevent it. Thus, in every view the want of steadiness can do no good, may do evil, and always leaves the conscience open to remorse!

Every man has a right to examine the sentiments and practices of his fellow Christians, to unite with those who in his view come the nearest to the word of God, and in a Christian-like manner to point out any error they may have embraced. This right no man can take from him, and in the proper exercise of it no one should interfere. He ought to render a reason, when properly asked of his faith and practice with meekness and fear; and may repel all censorious remark in the words of the apostle: "Who are you to pass judgement on the servant of another? It is before his own master that he stands or falls" (Romans 14:4).

But he ought to consider that while he believes his present religious profession to be agreeable to his Bible, he believes it to be the cause of truth; and the cause of truth is the cause of God. Will a man say there is little need of steadiness in his attention to the cause of his God?

Again, without steadiness no talents can make a professor of religion respectable. He has no weight as a professor of religion with those who know him. He may at times be admired, but he will not be esteemed. Whereas, very inferior talents with steadiness are not only respected, but their utility is felt and acknowledged. And what ought to alarm those who are the least inclined to unsteadiness is, that there is no setting a bound to it. Men may by degrees sink into such a state, as to imagine that, because they are disinclined, they are under no obligation to attend to God's worship, and that a great deal of *negligence* may consist with a very proper discharge of their duty! Thus, they go on till *admonition becomes useless*!

6
Applications

Encourage the Worship of God in Others
Many need it [encouragement] as much as you, and over some you may have a degree of influence. If you frequent the worship of God with seriousness, your example will produce some effect; it will be supposed you are in earnest, and that you see something important in religion. And in proportion to your situation, general character and abilities, the argument in its favour will be esteemed more or less conclusive. But besides, you may have it in your power to encourage the worship of God more immediately—those who have servants should remember they have souls, and while under their direction they ought not to deprive them of the means of receiving knowledge. The law of Moses held out an example worthy of the Christian's consideration: It made one day in the week a day of *rest* from all servile work. Nothing that could be avoided was done. Thus, an opportunity of worshipping God, and of acquiring some religious knowledge, was given to the lowest of the people. And shall Christians not encourage their servants to attend the worship of God, nor afford them opportunities of improvement in the great concerns of their eternal welfare? Where there are no means of obtaining information allowed, or but in a very limited degree, is it wonderful there should be no knowledge? Servants may have no inclination to cultivate their minds, it is true; but masters are not less bound at least to give them the opportunity, and set them the example. If the attempt fails, they have

done their duty. Many instances there have been of servants who have had reason to bless God for having guided them into the families of good men and women, where they were first led to a serious idea of God and his worship; and of masters who have had the pleasure of seeing the seeds of knowledge, which they helped to scatter, maturing into a humble and ardent piety! Let these things animate others to exertion.

How particularly does the same thing hold good respecting children! In a former part of this pamphlet, some notice has been taken of the influence of public worship on the rising generation, which, therefore, need not be here repeated; but if such be its influence, give it proper attention, that its effect may be as great as the use of means can make it. There is not a parent in the world who has any serious sense of religion, that would not rejoice in seeing his children, as they grow in years, grow in their attachment to God's worship. If negligent respecting it himself, he would still, with pleasure see them alert and diligent. But how can he expect this if he does not encourage them and go with them? Is it wonderful they should dislike the religious service they see a parent neglect? They soon learn to know that the worship of God is not a school for children, and they use the inconsistency of their friends as an apology for themselves. If brought up without religious habits and instruction, will they be the better for it? What reason have we to think they will? Let parents then endeavour to give pious sentiments an impression, by showing that they "love the habitation of your house, and the place where your glory dwells" (Psalm 26:8).

APPLICATIONS

Let Your Attendance Be Marked with Due Decorum

How many instances do our congregations exhibit of persons who habitually come *late*, as if their constant fear was least they should be confined too long. Some may be in such situations (not being their own masters) that they not know how to help it; others may accidentally be hindered from filling up their places in time; but because there is the possibility of an excuse in some cases, it does not follow that the negligent can always plead it. There is not one instance in many, where any defence of such conduct can be offered. The evil of a few examples in a congregation is great, and the indecorum too common to be much noticed; but considered in a true light it has an aspect few people will like to behold.

Most classes of Christians begin their service with some act of worship, others with reading a chapter of the Bible. Do you who are dilatory wish to be considered as thinking lightly of the *worship* or *word* of your God? But can you repel the charge, if it ever be made, on the ground of your regularly slighting that part in which God is particularly addressed or his word read? If indolence or carelessness be the cause, has it not produced a most serious and unpleasant appearance, when it leads you to act as if you thought the first parts of worship were of no consequence? And to whatever it be owing, where it is avoidable, there is no denying, that habitually slighting any part of worship must strike all who see it as a strange part of a Christian's character. What is its influence in families? Some are prevented from attending in time; others learn to imitate your conduct. Children copy the worst parts of their parents' example with the greatest exactness—and grow up in the opinion, that to neglect attending in time is no evil; besides the appearance it has, such ought to consider the disturbance they occasion by their untimely entrance. A well tutored mind will revolt at the thought of unnecessarily interrupting others in the most solemn of all employments.[1] And as the same right which one has to be late may be claimed by another, what would become of the worship of God were all to act in such a manner? What is to be judged when this late appearance in the house of God is owing to an attention to the business of this world? A case which too often happens.

Two things ask for your regard—the world and your God: Do you wish God should deal with you as you deal with him? Consider these things and learn to act as conscience dictates. Look through the religious societies with which you have been acquainted, and you will find, *with scarcely an exception*, that those who have been the greatest honour to the body, and added most to the edification of their brethren, attended on God's worship *steadily* and in *proper time*. There is often a striking analogy between people's manner in such things and their general religious character.

It deserves attention also, that when in a place of worship, the least we can do is not to disturb others. There are too many who make disturbing noises in various ways, which are severely felt as grievances by those around them, and they do not en-

---

[1] It has often been remarked, that during the time of prayer, many people seem, by their inattention and staring about, as if they were not at all engaged in it. It is hoped this charge does not belong to any of those who profess to consider religion as a serious concern. If it does, they ought to reflect on it, and be careful to give occasion for it no more. Ministers ought to remember, that it is important they should fulfill their part with as much propriety as they are able, that the attention of the hearers may be excited to their duty. And the people should recollect, that they should come to the house of prayer to worship God *in spirit and in truth*, and not to be merely present there, while their minds are wandering after anything that may attract their notice.

APPLICATIONS

deavour to break themselves of such habits. They ought, however, to recollect, that needlessly to interrupt their brethren is rudeness at least; that they lay themselves open to remarks they would by no means relish were they to know them; for who can expect that those who are disturbed should not censure? And if the matter was but considered and attended to by each, the evil would be cured. Ought the worship of God to be a noisy scene, to which people cannot attend with comfort? It may be said, why are such trifles mentioned? Because they are so often complained of as real evils. Would men take the hint, there would be no occasion to notice them; let them exercise a little common sense and reflection, and the business is done—"why do you not judge for yourselves what is right?" (Luke 12:57). Permit me to add:

In any alteration of your situations of life, keep an eye on the opportunity you will have of attending the worship of God; and let this consideration have some weight with you.

I will not say it will not add to your worldly interest to regard it, but it will to your happiness, if you are really concerned for the welfare of your souls. Take experience as your guide. How often has it happened, that when a person who appeared quite in earnest about religion, has been led into a situation where he could not attend on divine worship, or at least with any satisfaction, and has lost the society of those Christians with whom he associated and with whom he went to the house of God in company; that at first he felt uneasy like a stranger in a strange land: by and by, he was reconciled to live without the worship of God—mingled on the Lord's day, in the society and pleasures of those who fear not his name. Is it necessary to go any farther? Could anything result from hence but a cold indifference concerning those very things he once esteemed? Who would wish to be in such a state as this, that has ever "tasted that the Lord is good" (1 Peter 2:3)?

Or, suppose it does not come to this. Suppose in such a case a man retains his relish for religion, and will not unite with those whose company and manners might destroy any of its impressions; but should say of the house of God what the psalmist of old did of Jerusalem, "Let my tongue stick to the roof of my mouth, if I do not remember you, if I do not set Jerusalem above my highest joy" (Psalm 137:6), yet how painful his situation? How much does he lose in improvement and enjoyment? How does he seem to envy his brethren who are more favourably circumstanced? And could he have his choice it would be that he might have Christians for his friends, and God's worship for his consolation all the days of his life.

Here we may note, how important it is for young people who are about forming settlements for life, to consider how it will probably be with them. What a thought! To be united to a partner who shall be opponent to your best interests, who will tempt you to act contrary to the dictates of your conscience or ridicule and censure you for your perseverance? What a source of painful reflection! The person whom above all others you tenderly love, ignorant of God and of true happiness! What a prospect in educating a family! One parent planting, the other rooting up, or at least not watering religious instruction; while it receives only a partial assistance from divided example, and children are made parties in debates about it, instead of being taught by all the methods which authority and affection could use to *remember their Creator in the days of their youth* (Ecclesiastes 12:1)! What the apostle Paul said may in such cases be fairly applied "those who marry will have worldly troubles" (1 Corinthians 7:28). It is our duty to take into the account all the probable evils of our situation, and if we have not gone too far to admit of an alteration, to avoid the path of evident difficulty and sorrow.

Public Worship Is Not the Whole of Religion

It may be imagined by some from the stress here laid on attention to it, that it is made nearly the whole of religion. Far from it. It is a duty, an important duty, by some much neglected; and every Christian duty when it bespeaks our attention, should be pressed on the conscience with *earnestness*. But still it is only *one*, it does not make up for the want of justice, truth, benevolence, temperance, or purity. A diligent regard to the form is no substitute for the spirit of worship, nor for the trust in God for whatever we want. To make it properly useful, it requires us to be consistent characters, and that we should employ serious prayer to God, that his blessing may attend it. No man will ever arrive at that state of knowledge and experience, which the apostle Paul calls "the measure of the stature of the fullness of Christ" (Ephesians 4:13), merely by attending public worship. He must add to it, the study of his Bible, and attention to the state of his own heart. But the former is an encouragement to the latter and the last can hardly be without the first.

Public worship is valuable, as a means to an end; that end is an increase in knowledge, faith and holiness. The encouragement to cultivate it is great; for besides the motive before given, we may add, when Christians meet with proper dispositions for worship, there is not merely an assembly of men, the divine presence of their Saviour is with them. He said to his disciples, "where two or three are gathered in my name, there am I among them" (Matthew 18:20). And when he gave them his commission to preach the gospel in all nations, and to do and teach whatever he commanded, he added, "behold, I am with you always, to the end of the age" (Matthew 28:20). Can we desire more? "Let us not grow weary of doing good, for in due season we will reap, if we do not give up" (Galatians 6:9).

The third building of St. Mary's Baptist Chapel,
built during Kinghorn's ministry in 1812

Appendix 1

A Chronology of Joseph Kinghorn's Publications

1795 *A Defence of Infant Baptism, Its Best Confutation: Being A Reply to Mr. Peter Edwards's* Candid Reasons *for Renouncing the Principles of Anti-Paedo-Baptism, on his Own Ground* (Norwich)

1800 *Public Worship Considered and Enforced* (Norwich)

1803 *Address to a friend, who intends entering into church communion* (1st ed., Norwich)

1804 *Arguments, Chiefly from Scripture, Against the Roman Catholic Doctrine. In a Dialogue* (Norwich)

1808 *Observations on the Norfolk Benevolent Society of Protestant Dissenting Ministers; For the Relief of the Necessitous Widows and Orphans of Dissenting Ministers, and of Ministers who are by Age or Affliction Incapable of Public Service* (Norwich)

1811 *Serious Considerations Addressed to the House of Israel. The Substance of a Sermon, Delivered at the Jews' Chapel, December 16, 1810* (London: The London Society for Promoting Christianity Among the Jews)

1812 *The Miracles of Jesus not Performed by the Power of the Shem-Hamphorash. The Substance of a Sermon Preached at the Jews' Chapel, August 18, 1811, Being the Seventh Demonstration*

Sermon... With an Appendix on Jewish Traditions and the Perpetuity of the Law of Moses (London: The London Society for Promoting Christianity Among the Jews)

1813 *Address to a friend, who intends entering into church communion* (2nd ed., Norwich)

1813 *Scriptural Arguments for the Divinity of Christ, Addressed to the Serious Professors of Christianity* (1st ed., Norwich)

1814 *Advice and Encouragement to Young Ministers. Two Sermons addressed principally to the students of the two Baptist academies at Stepheny and at Bristol. The First Preached June 23, 1814, at the Rev. Dr. Rippon's Meeting, Carter-lane, Southwark; The Second, August 3, 1814, at the Rev. Dr. Ryland's, Broad Mead, Bristol* (Norwich)

1814 *Scriptural Arguments for the Divinity of Christ, Addressed to the Serious Professors of Christianity. Second Edition. With an Appendix, Containing Observations on the Rev. I. Perry's Letters to the Author* (2nd ed., Norwich)

1816 *Baptism, a Term of Communion at the Lord's Supper* (1st & 2nd eds., Norwich)

1816 *Fifth Report of the Committee of the Norfolk and Norwich Auxiliary Bible Society. September 1, 1816* (Norwich)

1817 *Practical Cautions to Students and Young Ministers. The Substance of a Sermon Preached at Bradford, in the County of York; At the Annual Meeting of the Northern Baptist Education Society, August 27, 1817* (Norwich)

1820 *A Defence of "Baptism a Term of Communion." In Answer to the Rev. Robert Hall's Reply* (Norwich)

1823 *The Arguments in Support of Infant Baptism, from the Covenant of Circumcision, Examined, and Shewn to Be Invalid* (London)

1824 *An Address to a Friend, on Church Communion: With An Appendix, Containing a Brief Statement of the Sentiments of the Baptists on the Ordinance of Baptism* (3rd ed., Norwich)

1824 Jacobo Robertson. *Clavis Pentateuchi: Sive Analysis Omnium Vocum Hebraicarum suo ordine in Pentateucho Moseos occurrentium, una cum versione Latina et Anglica; Notis Criticis et Philologicis Adjectis, in quibus, ex lingua Arabica, Judæorum Moribus, et Doctorum Itinerariis, plurium locorum S. S. Sensus Eruitur, novaque versione illustrator. In usum Juventutis Academicæ Edinburgenæ. Cui Præmittuntur Dissertationes Duæ; I. De antiquitate linguæ Arabicæ, ejusque conventientia cu, lingua Hebræa. II. De genuina punctorum vocalium antiquitate.* Edited by Joseph Kinghorn (Norwich)

1824 *A Brief Statement of the Sentiments of the Baptists on the Ordinance of Baptism* (Norwich; London)

1827 *Arguments Against the Practice of Mixed Communion, and in Support of Communion on the Plan of the Apostolic Church; With Preliminary Observations on Rev. R. Hall's Reasons for Christian, in Opposition to Party Communion* (London)

1827 *Sketch of the Life of the Rev. Isaac Slee; With an Extract from His Farewell Sermon, on His Resigning the Perpetual Curacy of Plumpton, in Cumberland, in Consequence of Becoming a Baptist* (London: Wightman and Cramp)

1829 *Remarks on a "Country Clergyman's Attempt to Explain the Nature of the Visible Church, the Divine Commission of the Clergy, &c." Being a Defence of Dissenters in General, and of Baptists in Particular; on New Testament Principles* (Norwich)

1831 *The Separate State.* In *The British Preacher, Under the Sanction of the Ministers Whose Discourses Appear in Its Pages*, I, 217-230 (London: Frederick Westley and A. H. Davis)

Appendix II

A Poem (1787)
by David Kinghorn

Peace, my soul, no more complain,
Jesus calls thee to His arms;
Rise above all grief and pain,
He shall keep thee free from harms.
Trust his promise, on him rest,
Freely he does for thee care;
Lean upon his loving breast—
In his heart thou hast a share.

Should found mothers monsters prove,
To the infants at their breast;
Yet th'eternal God of love,
Keeps the souls that on him rest.
Tho' the mountains should depart,
Hills be cast into the sea,
Still the kindness of his heart,
Yearns, provides, and cares for thee.

Why dispute his tender love,
While he such assurance gives?
Can his promise e'er remove?
Can'st thou die while Jesus lives?
Can'st thou want whil he supplies?

Can't thou fall while in his hand?
See, he listens to thy cries,
Guides, upholds, and makes thee stand.

Should both foes and fears assail,
Sickness waste, and rattling hail,
Clouds and darkness veil the skies;
On the stormy cloud he rides,
Swift pursues his wondrous way,
For thy safety still proves,
Turns thy darkness into day.

Mighty God, thou great and good!
All they creatures wait on Thee;
Thou provid'st them daily food;
Shall I doubt thy care for me?
Thou hast kept from dangers past,
Bid my troubled soul be still,
On Thee all my care I cast,
Patient wait my Father's will.

About the Editor

Baiyu Andrew Song (PhD cand., The Southern Baptist Theological Seminary) is the research assistant to the Director of the Andrew Fuller Centre for Baptist Studies, part-time lecturer at Redeemer University College and CCIC School of Theology. He is also the Executive Assistant at The Gospel Coalition Canada.

Scripture Index

Old Testament

Exodus
15:2 19
22:9-11 6
Deuteronomy
5:14-15 6
Job
10:2 24
Psalms
26:8 37
27:4 25
29:2 7
89:6-7 10
103:14 25
111:1 11

122:1 7
137:6 41
Proverbs
1:10 xxxi
15:23 24
Ecclesiastes
12:1 42
Isaiah
57:15 10
Micah
6:3 31
Malachi
1:13 7

New Testament

Matthew
- 16:14 23
- 17:4 12
- 18:20 43
- 28:20 43

Mark
- 8:34 23
- 9:5 12

Luke
- 4:16 6
- 9:23 23
- 9:33 12
- 12:57 40

John
- 9:4 28
- 14:6 19
- 17:3 19
- 18:36 13

Acts
- 4:12 19
- 11:42 7
- 16:30 14
- 17:2 7
- 22:7 7

Romans
- 14:4 33

1 Corinthians
- 7:28 42
- 14:3 21
- 16:2 7

2 Corinthians
- 2:16 29

Galatians
- 6:9 43

Ephesians
- 4:13 43

Colossians
- 3:16 7

2 Thessalonians
- 3:5 xxvii

1 Timothy
- 2:1 7
- 4:16 xxxiii

2 Timothy
- 3:17 15

Titus
- 2:11–14 xxxvi

Hebrews
- 10:25 .... 4, 7

1 Peter
- 2:3 41
- 5:7 24

2 Peter
- 1:16 29

Jude
- 20 22

Name	Date Read

H&E *Publishing*

WWW.HESEDANDEMET.COM

About Hesed & Emet Publishing

H&E Publishing is a Canadian evangelical publishing company located out of Peterborough, Ontario. We exist to provide Christ-exalting, Gospel-centred, and Bible-saturated content aimed to show God to be as glorious and worthy as He truly is.

Also Available from H&E

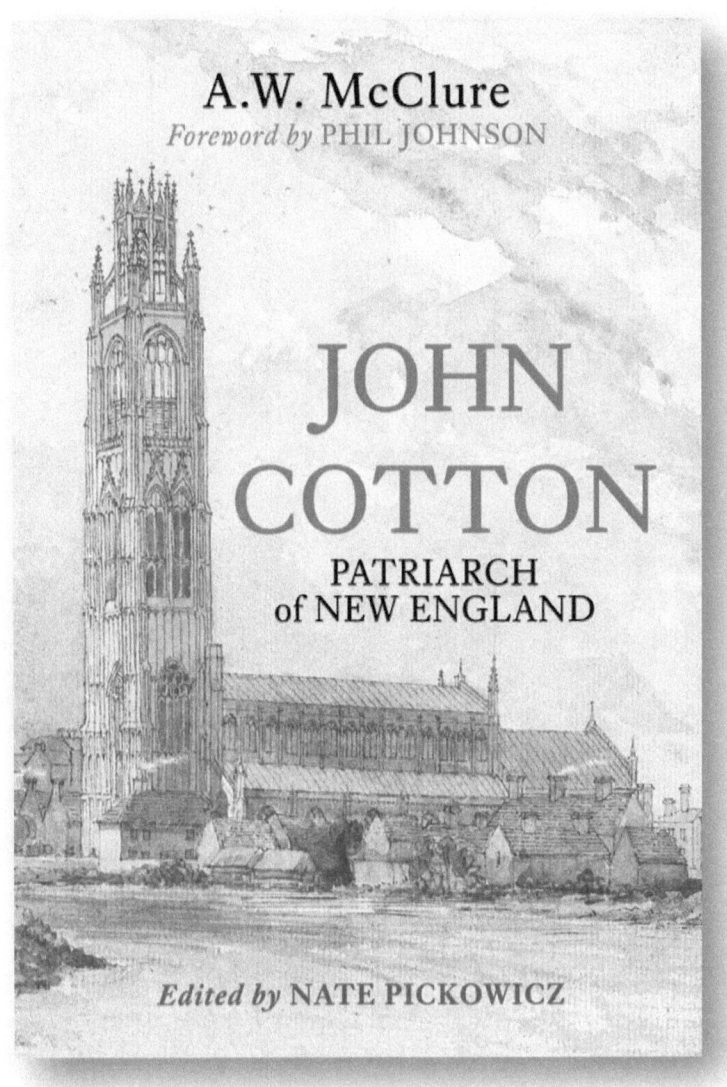

THE DIARY OF JAMES HINTON (1761–1823)

Introduced by MICHAEL A.G. HAYKIN
Edited by CHANCE FAULKNER

www.ingramcontent.com/pod-product-compliance
Lightning Source LLC
Chambersburg PA
CBHW020442090526
44586CB00045B/760